D0727530

BAPTISED WITH FIRE

God Promises Revival

A. Skevington Wood

Pickering & Inglis
LONDON · GLASGOW

ISBN 0 7208 0484 1
Cat. No. 01/0223

First published 1958
Paperback edition 1981

*This book was previously
issued under the title
AND WITH FIRE*

CONTENTS

PREFACE

I T is currently fashionable to assume that ours is the age of secularity. A determined attempt has been made through the media to persuade us that the tide of faith has ebbed, that the Christian Gospel is outdated and that the future lies with scientific materialism. The prophets of modern irreligion have decided that God is no longer a significant factor and that man is the measure and master of things.

As we enter the eighties, however, this secularist analysis is increasingly questioned. It is being realized at last that there is more to life than the human and the material. A growing awareness of the spiritual dimension is already a feature of this dawning decade. It is apparent, moreover, that if he is denied an authentic and positive experience of the supernatural in terms of the divine, man is liable to turn to the occult in an effort to meet what is a basic hunger for some sort of reality beyond the limits of the secular.

It is not therefore altogether surprising that in the sixties and seventies of this century the Christian Church has witnessed a movement of renewal in the Spirit on a world-wide scale. An aching void in the soul of secular man is being filled from a source in God Himself. Historians may well reach the conclusion that the formidable bastions of godless materialism were breached and its citadel threatened during the very period when as Christians some have been tempted almost to despair. Certainly God has not left himself without witness even in the difficult and testing days through which we are called to live.

Yet having recognized that the outlook for God's people is not as gloomy as some may have imagined, it must be added that revival still tarries. Gratitude to God for all the encouraging signs of our times in the quickening of the Spirit, in a renewed interest in evangelism and in a genuine concern to grasp the biblical principles of church growth, should not mislead us into supposing that we are either into or even on the verge of a general recovery of nerve within the Church of Christ. When we consider the darker side of the contemporary scene — the insidious inroads of acquisitiveness, the alarming polarization of society in terms of class or racial distinctions, the upsurge of violence and terrorist tactics, the steep decline in personal and more particularly sexual morals and, with all, the 'contagion of the world's slow stain' impairing the testimony of the Church itself — we are disposed to echo the lamentation of Jeremiah that 'the harvest is past, the summer is ended, and we are not saved' (Jeremiah 8:20).

However, such an attitude of cautious realism is justified only if it compels us to enquire of the Lord in order to find out why revival is delayed. It is good that we should face the uncomfortable fact that, despite many zealous and even frantic efforts, the Church has not yet succeeded in rehabilitating itself, let alone in redeeming the world. But it is bad that we should on this account sit back and resign ourselves either to the false and fatal fallacy that God is unable to intervene or to the equally unwarranted and perilous assumption that He does not desire or design to refresh His chosen with a display of His renovating power. Instead, we should be constrained to ask, as Jeremiah did, 'Is there no balm in Gilead; is there no physician there? Why then is not the health of the daughter of my people recovered?' (Jeremiah 8:22).

Only a concentrated scrutiny of the Scriptures as they relate to God's gift of revival will furnish an adequate answer to such a pertinent enquiry and indicate the path which the Lord is calling His Church to tread as we negotiate the uncharted eighties. This book is the fruit of a previous attempt at an undertaking of that sort. It was shortly after Dr Billy Graham's memorable crusades here in Britain in 1954 and 1955 that I was first led to search the Word together with the records of past revivals in order to discover what are the regulative principles underlying these potent movements of the Spirit. Since then I have sought to pursue the investigation even further. It has been a chastening as well as an illuminating project, and I continue to thank God for the measure in which my own ministry has been enriched and enlarged because He has dealt with me in the well-springs of the soul. If what is set down here should be the means of guiding others into the same experience it will have achieved its primary objective.

These chapters do not pretend to present an exhaustive and systematic theological treatment of the subject with which they deal. They are addressed to the ordinary Christian reader and are cast in the form of simple expository and inspirational messages on the theme of revival. Some have actually been delivered as such and no doubt still betray the symptoms of direct speech. Others originally appeared as published articles. All stand in debt to the researches of others in this field and, whilst saluting those from whom I have freely borrowed, I must add a special word of appreciation to the Evangelical Library in London for permission to consult at leisure the very valuable collection of rarer volumes housed there.

The messages have been arranged in what would appear to be the most logical order, but since they represent separate entities there is some unavoidable overlapping. The author is even more conscious of their imperfections than the most critical reader will be, although at the same time gratified that a new edition has been called for. His heartfelt prayer still is that through these pages the quickening Word may be uttered and the people of God baptised once more with the Holy Spirit and with fire (Matthew 3:11).

A. Skevington Wood

Cliff College,
   Calver,
      Sheffield.

July, 1980

CHAPTER I

THE PROMISE OF REVIVAL

'Prove Me now herewith, saith the Lord of hosts, if I will not open you the windows of heaven, and pour you out a blessing, that there shall not be room enough to receive it.'
—Malachi 3. 10

DWIGHT L. Moody often used to wonder why it was that revivals were looked for everywhere but in the realm of religion. Shop keepers are always hoping for a revival of demand. The captains of commerce confidently anticipate a revival of trade. Industrial establishments await a revival of business. Political parties are perpetually sanguine about the prospects of revival. And those whose domestic finances have reached the stage of embarrassment are constantly exercising a Micawber-like expectancy that something will turn up. In all departments of life we find that men are very anxious for a revival in the things that concern them most. Why then is it that God's people are not equally and indeed surpassingly agitated about spiritual revival? Should not every child of God be praying for and earnestly desiring a revival of righteousness in this sin-soiled world today? Should not the Christian Church continually entertain great expectations of Pentecostal renewal?

Such, however, is all too obviously not the case. The hunger for revival is not noticeably sharp. The thirst is not prostratingly insatiable. It cannot be said that we are weary with our groaning or that tears are our food night and day as we plead for the blessing. On the contrary, despite the concern of a faithful remnant, the Church as a whole is largely indifferent to the urgency of this issue.

Revival ought to be the paramount preoccupation of God's children. Instead it is relegated to an insignificant backwater. It should fill the centre of our total concern: in fact it is pushed unceremoniously into the margin.

What is the reason for this lack of conviction about revival? How can the people of the saints of the Most High be so apathetic in such a vital matter? We must allow, of course, for the infiltration of Satan's devices even amongst the chosen of God. It is the devil's design to keep us in a state of slumber. His trump card is to lull believers into a false complacency. But apart from this deliberate strategy of the Wicked One and the unceasing proneness of Christians to lapse into lethargy, there does appear to be a further cause behind this current careless-ness in respect of revival. It is this: that there are many within the Church of Christ who do not really believe in revival at all. They do not deny that God quickened His people at Pentecost, but they feel that such a miracle was unique and unrepeatable. Or, if they are persuaded to recognise the phenomenon of revival as recurring in history, they argue that it has now spent itself and that we cannot look for any further awakening. It is said that the times have waxed too late and gross for us to hope for renewal now, or that living as many suppose we do in the last age no revival can be looked for until the Lord returns. These views are seriously expressed by a con-siderable body of opinion today.

What is the truth of the situation? Is revival still God's will? Have the Church and the world declined beyond the limit of recovery? Can we no longer hope for seasons of spiritual refreshment? Is there anything anywhere to encourage us to expect or pray and labour for a revival of religion? The answer, of course, lies deep in God's unalterable Word. We may confidently wait and work for further manifestations of Pentecostal outpouring because God Himself has assured it. 'What are the prospects of revival?' asked Arthur Wallis of an aged servant of the Lord. 'They are as bright as the promises of God,' was his worthy reply. That is the sure foundation for faith in the reality of revival. Dr. A. T. Pierson counted over thirty-thousand promises in the Book of God and a surprising proportion of them refer to spiritual renewal. Not one of them has been cancelled. God always remembers His holy promise. He faithfully fulfils all that He has covenanted to perform. 'Wait for the promise of the Father' our Lord commanded the apostles before He ascended up on high (Acts 1. 4): the selfsame injunction is repeated in each successive age of the Church, for unless the gift of Pentecost is received afresh there can be no blessing or power in the life of the individual believer or of the Christian community. 'Many men consider an old promise obsolete though unfulfilled,' wrote Ernest Baker of Cape Town in *The Revivals of the Bible*. 'But it is not so with God. The promises of revival still hold good.'

We may therefore rest assured that God is always ready to honour His Word by sending revival. He is only hampered by our failure to comply with His conditions. There is no invasion or infringement of His sovereignty in this circumstance. Many of God's promises are conditional: there is no reflection on His omnipotence if He withholds the bestowal until the terms have been met. The entry of the Israelites into the Promised Land itself was postponed for this very reason. 'After the number of the days in which ye searched the land, even forty days, each day for a year, shall ye bear your iniquities, even forty years, and ye shall know My breach of promise' (Numbers 14. 34). God held aloof from His people until they obeyed His orders. So He does still in the realm of revival.

The familiar and much-quoted verse from Malachi
3. 10 contains a sure promise of God's abundant blessing.
It is as if He challenges the faith of His children by
requiring them to put Him to the test. Let them imagine
the most copious outpouring their minds can conceive,
and He will do for them 'exceeding abundantly above all
that they ask or think' (Ephesians 3. 20). But all this
royal largesse is only to be distributed when God's people
have conceded His request. 'Bring ye all the tithes into
the storehouse, that there may be meat in Mine house.'
Only as they bring forth fruits meet for repentance will
God visit them with fruit from heaven. The conditional
nature of the promise is clear from verse 7. 'Even from
the days of your fathers ye are gone away from Mine
ordinances and have not kept them. Return unto Me,
and I will return unto you, saith the Lord of hosts.'
(cf. Zechariah 1. 3).

This passage from Malachi thus enshrines the promise
of revival. It speaks first of THE CERTAINTY OF IT.
There is no hesitation in this assurance. God Himself
firmly declares that it shall be so. What can withstand
His Word? When God utters His voice the performance
of what He proposes is ensured. That is why the promises
and the prophecies concerning revival merge into one
another. There is little distinction between them. God's
promise to revive His Church is equivalent to a prophecy
that His Church shall be revived. And God's prophecy
of revival, since it issues from the Almighty One, is
equivalent to a gracious promise

We are almost overwhelmed by the multiplicity of
Scripture assertions of this certainty. That is why Arthur
Wallis can devote two-hundred and fifty pages (the extent
of his invaluable book *In the Day of Thy Power*) to a close
examination of 'the inescapable Biblical authority for
such "times of refreshing from the presence of the Lord,"

and the conditions upon which God still comes, as in Apostolic days with "mighty signs and wonders, by the power of the Spirit of God".' We can do no more than turn up one or two of these many references which unmistakably indicate that the promises of revival before the Lord's Return are as definite as those of the Second Advent itself. There is Isaiah 44. 3: 'For I will pour water upon him that is thirsty, and floods upon the dry ground: I will pour My Spirit upon thy seed, and My blessing upon thine offspring.' There is Jeremiah 33. 3, 6: 'Call unto Me, and I will answer thee, and shew thee great and mighty things, which thou knowest not. . . . Behold I will bring it health and cure, and I will cure them, and reveal unto them the abundance of peace and truth.' There is Joel 2. 28, 29: 'And it shall come to pass afterward, that I will pour out of My Spirit upon all flesh; and your sons and your daughters shall prophesy, your old men shall dream dreams, your young men shall see visions: and also upon the servants and upon the handmaids in those days will I pour out of My Spirit.' Referring to Joel's prophecy John Fletcher of Madeley commented: 'A blessed promise of which our Lord gave an earnest on the day of Pentecost when He sent a glorious shower on His little vineyard, a pledge of the mighty rivers of righteousness which will by and by cover the earth as the waters cover the sea.'

The New Testament is equally rich in revival assurances. Our Lord Himself spoke of a present ingathering. 'Say not ye, There are yet four months, and then cometh the harvest? behold, I say unto you, Lift up your eyes, and look on the fields; for they are white already to harvest' (John 4. 35) Peter at Pentecost appealed to the sure word in Joel and plainly claimed 'this is that' (Acts 2. 16). By the inspiration of the Holy Ghost it was given him to see that the 'former and latter rain' of the prophetic Scriptures was to fall in the age of the Church. Again, in the sermon at the Beautiful Gate of the Temple, Peter exhorted the multitude thus: 'Repent ye therefore, and be converted, that your sins may be blotted out, when (or so that) the times of refreshing shall come from the presence of the Lord' (Acts 3. 19). What follows makes it evident that such 'times of refreshing' arrive *after* Pentecost and *before* the Lord's Return.

The promises of God's Word make it infallibly certain that when His people turn to Him He will in the time that He appoints turn once again to them. Revival is not a doubtful possibility: it is a firm inevitability when the way is cast up and the season is due. There should be no reservations in our prayers for revival. We must not say, 'Lord, if it be Thy will, quicken Thy Church.' It *is* His will. He has told us no less. We should therefore go boldly to the throne of grace and plead the promises. We must believe not only that God can but that He will send revival. Any reticence is dishonouring to God. It suggests that He is either unable or unwilling to implement His Word. Prevailing faith will dare to confront the Lord with His own assurances and in response to His own invitation will put Him to the proof. It was altogether in this triumphant spirit that John Oxtoby—'praying Johnny' as he was nicknamed—besought God to bless in the days of the Primitive Methodist awakening. 'Thou munna make a feal o' me,' was the burden of one of his hedgeback petitions, overheard by a passer-by; 'I told them at Bridlington Thou was gannin to revive Thy work, and Thou mun dea so or I shall never be able to show my face among them again.' Nothing pleases our heavenly Father better than to see His promises put into circulation; He loves to see His children bring them up to Him, and say, 'Lord, do as Thou hast said'.

This passage from Malachi has more to say about the

promise of revival. It speaks of THE SUFFICIENCY OF IT. God tells His people that the outpoured blessing will be so abundant 'that there shall not be room enough to receive it.' Just as 'the windows of heaven were opened' in Noah's flood, to release a deluge of wrath (Genesis 7. 11) so they will be opened yet again to release such a torrent of grace that they will have to pull down their barns and build greater in a vain attempt to contain it. As Edward Pococke explained it, the verse means: 'I will pour out on you such a blessing as shall be not enough only, and such as shall be sufficient, but more and more than enough.' It will be like the gathering of spoil in the valley of Berachah, more than can be carried away (2 Chronicles 20. 25).

Revival is only to be measured by the standard of God's inexhaustible power. It may be expected to reach Pentecostal proportions. On the first Whit Sunday no less than three thousand souls were swept into the Kingdom within the space of a few brief hours. Think of it! Weigh the excited estimate of William Arthur in his classic, *The Tongue of Fire*. 'Three thousand men permanently raised from death in sin to a life of holiness! Three thousand sinners converted into saints! Three thousand new-made saints enabled day by day to walk in the fear of God, and in the comfort of the Holy Ghost! Three thousand of our brethren, weak, sinful by nature, open to the temptings of Satan even as we are, maintaining a life in the body which almost surpasses belief, so is it marked with goodness and purity!' That thrilling epitome of the incalculable consequences of Pentecost reminds us of a sufficiency which is spiritual as well as numerical.

The records of subsequent revivals amply substantiate the fulfilment of this prophetic promise. Pentecost was but the beginning. The incredible continued to happen.

And from time to time throughout the course of Christian history the awakenings of the Holy Spirit have affected whole towns, whole districts, whole countries and even whole continents. 'Who hath heard such a thing? who hath seen such things? Shall the earth be made to bring forth in one day? or shall a nation be born at once?' (Isaiah 66. 8). Concerning the Scottish Reformation Kirkton wrote: 'The whole nation was converted by lump. Lo! here a nation born in one day: yea, moulded into one congregation, and sealed as a fountain with a solemn oath and covenant.'

The statistics of revival afford an encouraging study. They show what wonders God can perform. Let us review the figures for the 1859 awakening alone. They are impressive indeed. According to the careful researches of Dr. J. Edwin Orr the number of converts reached 100,000 in Ireland, the same total in Wales (representing one-tenth of the population), at least 300,000 in Scotland and at least 650,000 in England. The simultaneous movement in America, which extended over half a century, can be called without exaggeration the 'Million-fold Revival' since more than 1,000,000 were touched by it. These are conservative estimates, based on the returns of Church membership relative to the period. They speak for themselves of the sufficiency of revival.

But the influence of a spiritual renascence cannot be gauged solely by such a census as the foregoing. We have to take into account the astonishing spread of the quickening flame. The way in which the display of Divine power permeated every level of society has to be considered. The effect of revival upon the various departments of communal life needs to be included in our survey. And most of all the spiritual repercussions of such a season demand assessment, insofar as that is in any measure possible. An honest enquiry into all these factors as evidenced in the revivals of past centuries more than justifies the promise of sufficiency. There are no restrictions to what God can accomplish. The straitening is in ourselves, not in Him.

This passage from Malachi has something yet again to say about the promise of revival. It speaks of THE SATISFACTION OF IT. Fulness cannot fail to satisfy. The picture here is of repletion and more than repletion. A blessing bigger than can be housed must needs spell contentment to the recipients. Mouths are filled with laughter and tongues with singing. The assurance of the Psalmist is corroborated in actual experience. 'They shall be abundantly satisfied with the fatness of Thy house; and Thou shalt make them drink of the river of Thy pleasures' (Psalm 36. 8).

The Scripture consistently speaks of this profound satisfaction that revival brings to the people of God in terms of the replenishment of rain. We in the West find it hard to enter into the oriental appreciation of the merciful gift of rain. In the last of a fascinating series of B.B.C. talks on the Bushmen of the Kalahari Desert, Laurens van der Post, the distinguished explorer and writer, told of the coming of the rains to the interior of Africa. He happened to be with one of the lost tribes at the very season. For many long dry months they had been yearning for the refreshment of a life-giving shower and when at length it came they celebrated the event with song and dance. Everything seemed new and different afterwards and hope and joy returned once more. The note of deep satisfaction was generally apparent. So God promises to rain righteousness upon His waiting people and the fulfilment of His gracious Word brings unutterable peace. 'I will cause the shower to come down in his season; there shall be showers of blessing' (Ezekiel 34. 26) and with them a sweet content. It arises out of the believer's renewed assurance that God has not failed to honour His promise.

> "O living Stream, O gracious Rain,
>   None wait for Thee, and wait in vain."

What then is the conclusion of the whole matter? It is this. Since God promises revival, Christians must expect it. There must be no more rationalisation of mediocrity. There must be no more questioning whether God wills to bless. The prayer of faith must ask, seek, knock. The annals of the past unite to testify that revival has only come where it has been believed in and waited for, even if only by the faithful few. The promises of God are given us to claim, not to ignore. 'Indeed, what is the use of a promise—how can it be of any service, except as it is held and pleaded in prayer?' enquired John G. Lorimer, in a paragraph that we shall do well to ponder as we leave this subject. 'We would not have presumed to ask God for great revivals of religion had He not condescended to promise: but having promised what is our duty but to believe His Word, and live in the lively expectation that the prediction will be accomplished? It is thus that we honour God and obtain the thing promised. As there is nothing which honours Him more than fully, cheerfully, unreservedly believing His Word; so there is nothing in return which He more honours than this believing. He blesses it with success.'

CHAPTER II

THE NECESSITY OF REVIVAL

'O Lord, revive Thy work in the midst of the years, in the midst of the years make known; in wrath remember mercy.'
—Habakkuk 3. 2

THIS is a cry to God for revival at a time when revival seems remote and unlikely. The prophet Habakkuk applies to the Almighty for relief 'in the midst of the years'. That is when faith and hope dwindle. That is when the possibility of quickening appears to be infinitesimal. That is when its necessity is scarcely acknowledged. But that is when supplication must be intensified and the people of God besiege the gates of heaven with all-prevailing prayer.

As Sir George Adam Smith has reminded us in his exposition of this portion of the Word, we, too, live among the nameless years. We feel them about us and are numbed by their passivity. The times in which we are set are undistinguished by the more spectacular workings of God's Spirit. It is more than nineteen centuries now since the revelation of the Father in the flesh of His Son, since the purchase of a world's salvation by the shedding of Calvary blood, since the signal enduement of the Church with power on the Day of Pentecost. Those stirring manifestations of the primitive period of the faith seem distant indeed and we remain for the most part unmoved by the expectation of the approaching End. We stand 'in the midst of the years' and the extremities of our Lord's First and Second Advents are far removed from our consideration. It is the midnight hour between even and morning when, as our Lord Himself has taught

us, it is imperative that we should watch lest coming
suddenly He find us sleeping (cf. Mark 13. 35, 36).

It is precisely at such a perilous juncture that believers
require to be convinced afresh concerning the necessity
of revival. They need to be stirred from listless indifference. Nothing is more calculated to effect such an
awakening than the reminder that Pentecost was not a
once-for-all occurrence but a continuously repeatable
miracle. The story of Acts Two is widely known amongst
Christian people but sadly misunderstood. It is wrongly
regarded as an isolated occasion. In one sense, of course,
the events of the first Whitsuntide were unique and
incapable of repetition. The initial effusion of the Holy
Spirit marked a distinct epoch in sacred history. There
can never again be an original gift of the Spirit to the
Church. But the error into which so many believers fall
is the supposition that the experience of Pentecost cannot
be renewed in succeeding generations. It is felt that God
has exhausted the dynamic that produced the miracle of
revival. They labour under the mistaken impression that
God has, so to speak, shot His bolt in that respect. The
consequence is that the idea of revival recedes from view.
It is no longer regarded as necessary since it cannot be
admitted within the bounds of possibility. The assumption thereupon gains ground that Zion is to be enlarged
only in a silent and gradual manner by the consecrated
efforts of devoted Christian workers. The passionate
prayer, 'O Lord, revive Thy work in the midst of the
years' is no more heard and for lack of vision the people
ultimately perish.

An elementary acquaintance with Church History
would dispel such a regrettable and indeed tragic
misconception. It would reveal beyond denial that God
has from time to time refreshed His heritage with outpourings of the Spirit almost as remarkable as Pentecost.

And what He has done in the past, He can do again
today. 'Revival in our time' is not just a convenient
caption. It represents a Divine reality through the
operation of the quickening Spirit. As D. L. Moody
used to insist, Pentecost was but a specimen day. O that
such days might be seen in our midst once again! There
is nothing we need more.

Revival must be considered primarily as A NECESSITY
IN THE WILL OF GOD. The ultimate source of spiritual
quickening lies in the nature of the Father. He is life
and He brings life. Revival flows from what God is and
what He does. As David Matthews has observed, 'Divine
movements have their birthplace in the heart of Deity.'

Two of the many Scriptural titles of God will serve to
indicate the relationship between revival and the Divine
nature. Perhaps the most typical term for the identifi-
cation of God in the Old Testament is the adjective
'living'. 'But the Lord is the true God, He is the living
God, and an everlasting King' (Jeremiah 10. 10). The
Hebrew for 'living' occurs more than sixty times in the
formal oath which contains the name of God, although
in our English translation it is rendered as a verb (cf. 'As
the Lord liveth' Judges 8. 19). It is for the living God
that the Psalmist thirsts (Psalm 42. 2). It is the living God
who drives out Israel's enemies (Joshua 3. 10). Now it is
by virtue of this characteristic that God is the initiator of
revival. He is the only source of life, whether physical
or spiritual. It was He Who 'formed man of the dust of
the ground, and breathed into his nostrils the breath of
of life; and man became a living soul' (Genesis 2. 7). It is
He who brings new souls to birth and calls men from the
death of sin to the life of righteousness. The living God
is the life-giving God and nowhere is that quality dis-
played more markedly than in the phenomenon of
revival. It is the outcome of a Divine necessity. Because

God is the God of life He must needs convey life wherever He works.

Another title by which God is known in Scripture is 'Almighty.' As H. F. Stevenson points out in his study of sacred nomenclature, this is a most inadequate rendering which fails to capture the profound implication of the Hebrew *El Shaddai*. The name suggests at once the sufficiency, the bountifulness and the consolation of God. Unlimited resources, abundant supply and tender comfort are implied. The initial occurrence of this term in Scripture underlines its distinctive significance. It is in Genesis 17. 1, where Abraham has reached the end of his own abilities insofar as the continuation of the chosen race is concerned and can only rely upon the never-failing fulness of God. It is then that the Lord appears to Abraham and says: 'I am the Almighty God; walk before Me, and be thou perfect. And I will make My covenant between Me and thee, and will multiply thee exceedingly.' It is because the God with whom we have to do is this kind of God that revival is a Divine necessity. He is 'the Enough God'. His grace can match every human situation. His power is inexaustible. His springs never run dry. Being what He is He must needs refresh His people from time to time with beneficent showers.

If revival is the expression of God's nature, it is also the fulfilment of His holy purpose. It is a necessity in His will. He decrees and it is done. He speaks and the blessing follows. However much we may take to heart those unequivocal passages of Scripture which urge the essential conditions which govern the gift of God, we must not suppose that they detract even in the slightest degree from the sole sovereignty of Him who is the supreme Disposer of all things. He has predestined all who will believe 'unto the adoption of children by Jesus Christ to Himself, according to the good pleasure of His will' (Ephesians 1. 5). The Divine necessity of revival is intimately linked with the Father's eternal covenant with the Son to give Him the heathen for His inheritance and the uttermost parts of the earth for His possession. 'I have sworn by Myself, the word is gone out of My mouth in righteousness, and shall not return, That unto Me every knee shall bow, every tongue shall swear' (Isaiah 45. 23). As Philippians 2. 10 reveals, that universal purpose of God will be accomplished in Christ His Son. The final success of the Gospel is assured in the glorious mission of our Emmanuel. It is His reward, guaranteed to Him by a Divine oath. It will be completed at His Return, but it will be prepared as in each successive generation God adds to His Church such as shall be saved.

Here, then, is the basic reason why revival is a necessity. It is in the counsel of God's will. The Word assures us that God has not only promised to bless, but has undertaken to bless. We are not only told that it shall be: we are taught that it must be. And as in this matter God has, 'made known unto us the mystery of His will, according to His good pleasure which He hath purposed in Himself' (Ephesians 1. 9), we can only bow before it and accept His wise decree.

Revival must be considered again as A NECESSITY FOR THE LIFE OF THE CHURCH. Pentecost is not a luxury. It is an absolute essential. Without the continuous infilling of the Spirit neither the individual believer nor the Christian community can maintain life and effectively witness in the world. We may not always see the need for renewal but we nevertheless stand in need of it perpetually. When it has ceased we are restricted until it is restored. When it is flourishing we can only prosper as it is sustained. The Church is thus always dependent upon revival. It must pray either to be revived or to stay revived.

As we analyse the contemporary situation we are driven to the unwelcome but salutary conclusion that revival is not something we have and must seek to keep but something we lack and must plead to receive. There can be no serious disagreement with such an appraisal, however unpalatable it may be. The Spirit is saying to the Church of today what He said to Sardis in the first Christian century: 'I know thy works, that thou hast a name that thou livest, and art dead' (Revelation 3. 1). Never before did the Church boast such organisation and machinery. Never before did the Church devise such ambitious schemes for evangelisation and extension. Never before did the Church aim to make such an impact upon surrounding society. But what has been the net result of all this multifarious expenditure of energy? Our condition is much what it was twenty-five years ago. We seem to be condemned to a treadmill: all our apparently progressive activity is in fact advancing us not a whit. At last we are beginning to realise that mere methods, mere schemes, mere endeavours will not of themselves produce the desired effect. Without the flow of the Spirit they may prove as futile as the frenzied activism of Elijah's rivals on Mount Carmel. 'And they cried aloud, and cut themselves after their manner with knives and lancets, till the blood gushed out upon them. And it came to pass, when midday was past, and they prophesied until the time of the offering of the evening sacrifice, that there was neither voice, nor any to answer, nor any that regarded' (I Kings 18. 28, 29).

We are rapidly realizing the bankruptcy of pragmatism within the Church. It is being admitted on all hands that the hour has come to 'cast our deadly doing down.' It is achieving nothing for it lacks the touch of Pentecost. That is the supreme need of the Church today—a fresh baptism of the Holy Spirit. Revival is a necessity to the

Church. As Dr. Stanley Jones once wrote in *The Christ of Every Road*, 'The Church is not living in Pentecost. It is living between Easter and Pentecost. Easter stands for a life wrought out and offered. Pentecost stands for life appropriated and lived to its full. The Church stands hesitant between the two. Hesitant, hence comparatively impotent. If the Church would move up to Pentecost, nothing could stop it—NOTHING.' Those are provocatively relevant words. They place an unerring finger upon our present deficiency. Here is the source of our prevalent failure. Here is the cause of our carnal futility. And here too is the key to spiritual success. The Church must move up to Pentecost.

A Bishop who was deeply concerned about the need for spiritual improvement in one of the parishes of his diocese, wrote to the incumbent and said: 'Dear Vicar, I propose to come to your parish to conduct a quiet day.' But the Vicar, who knew the condition of his people all too well, wrote back and said: 'Dear Bishop, It is not a quiet day we want in this parish but an earthquake.' That is the universal need of the modern Church. Only a Pentecostal earthquake will shake us into vitality once again.

'Without the manifest presence of the Holy Ghost any church is a failure' declared Dr. P. F. Bresee. 'It may be a great machine, wheels within wheels, but it is without life and power. Such an organisation bears the same relation to the Church of Christ that a dead body bears to a man. A dead body is organised matter; it is the form, and has the appearance of a man, but for all purposes for which a man was created it is a useless thing. So with a church. It is organised humanity; in many respects it looks like the real thing; but for the purposes for which the Church was called into being, it is utterly useless. It may amuse, entertain, instruct men, but to lift men out of their sins and take sin out of them it is powerless to do.' Only revival can transform the sham into the reality. Only Pentecost can impart life to the dead. 'Come from the four winds, O breath, and breathe upon these slain, that they may live' (Ezekiel 37. 9).

Revival must be considered lastly as A NECESSITY TO THE REDEMPTION OF THE WORLD. For God's plan of salvation for mankind operates through the Church. He chooses to bring deliverance to the race through the remnant. But if His Israel apostasizes from Him, there can be no hope for the world until His own are restored. It is by reviving the Church that God aims to rescue the wandering sheep outside the fold. That is why Moody declared, 'I had rather wake a slumbering Church than a slumbering world.' It was not that he shrank from the latter assignment, but he knew that it was an impossibility until first the people of God were roused

Few are likely to dispute the assertion that the world sorely needs redemption. Things have reached such an ugly pass in this atomic era that the clamant urgency of the situation can hardly be overlooked. A new and terrible sword of Damocles hangs over our whole civilisation. Men's hearts are failing them for fear and the future seems grim indeed. The moving words of Sir Winston Churchill in the House of Lords in 1955, as he disclosed the defencelessness of man against the hydrogen bomb, voiced the pathos of the multitudes who faced the oncoming years with bewildered misgiving. 'I find it poignant,' he said, 'to look at youth in all its ardour, and most of all to watch little children at play, and I wonder what will lie before them if God wearies of mankind.' Should the Lord cast off for ever, then our world is doomed indeed.

The prophet Habakkuk lived in an age of upheaval like our own. He knew where hope was to be sought.

'O Lord, I have heard Thy speech, and was afraid: O Lord, revive Thy work in the midst of the years, in the midst of the years make known; in wrath remember mercy.' There lies the only exit from our impasse. Man has got himself into a mess, but he cannot get himself out. Only God can do that and our prayer must be that in the midst of His just anger He will deal graciously with us. 'I see coming chaos as clearly as the shepherds saw the star of Bethlehem,' writes Roger Babson. 'Only one thing will stop this coming chaos—a sweeping spiritual awakening.' 'We live in a nightmare world,' says William Ward Ayer. 'Time is running out! We are near the end! Hell is seething up out of the pit. Death is preparing for its great carnage. If Almighty God does not intervene, human beings will be dying like flies—millions of burned and blackened corpses, the victims of a new plague—the burning hell of the hydrogen bomb!'

There is an inescapable challenge to believers in these shattering circumstances of our time. How shall we escape the rebuke of the Most High if we neglect to plead for revival and point sinners to their Saviour in these days of doom? Indifference to such vital matters is always to be deplored, but in an age of crisis like our own it is criminally inexcusable. 'If thou forbear to deliver them that are drawn unto death, and those that are ready to be slain; if thou sayest, Behold we knew it not; doth not He that pondereth the heart consider it? and He that keepeth thy soul, doth not He know it? and shall not He render to every man according to his works?' (Proverbs 24. 11, 12). We require to recapture the passion for the lost that stamped the witness of our forefathers. The prospects of many thousands heading for an eternity without Christ should stir us to fervent prayer and unremitting zeal in commending Him to others. We should devote our every sacred moment to this imperative enterprise, lest it should be said that our lack of concern has hindered that Pentecostal bestowal which alone can redeem the world.

There is a solemn admonition in the comment of Frank C. Laubach in his book, *Channels of Spiritual Power*. 'While we slumbered, other people were hard at work. While we failed to go all-out in spreading the Christian Gospel, energetic evangelists of a false, communistic, atheistic, materialistic gospel have gone all-out to sow their ideas everywhere. The world is like an overripe fruit. It is going to be evangelized to something. If Christianity is not energetic and virile enough to capture the world, something else will be. It may be Communism.' Such a realisation as that should stimulate the consecrated endeavour of Christians everywhere. We need to pray for revival whilst we toil in evangelism. Waiting and working will be wedded in this overriding preoccupation with a world's salvation.

So much, then, for the necessity of revival. Let us never again allow Satan to persuade us that Pentecost is not needed any more. Remember the stirring peroration of John Bonar's great sermon on revival. It is not only full of blessing, he argues, but absolutely necessary. 'The work of revival must begin, and must go on. People speak of it as a thing which may or may not be, which though they distantly wish they can yet do without. Why, what do people mean? What is a revival but multiplied conversions? What is a revival but living Christianity? If we can do without conversion; if we can do without Christ; if we can do without regeneration; if our children can do without these, if our friends and neighbours can do without these, then may we do without revival. But if conversion is necessary; if regeneration is necessary; if salvation is necessary, then is a revival necessary.'

CHAPTER III

THE CONDITIONS OF REVIVAL

'If My people, which are called by My name, shall humble themselves, and pray, and seek My face, and turn from their wicked ways; then will I hear from heaven, and will forgive their sin, and will heal their land.' —2 Chronicles 7. 14

THIS is the classic verse of the Old Testament Scriptures with reference to the way in which revival is granted. It has provided the text for many a sermon. It has been appealed to by many a prophetic leader as he sought to rouse the dormant Church of his day. It has been marked in many a devout believer's Bible. More than most verses of the enduring Word it has spoken to those who yearned for revival. It still has much to tell us today.

Kierkegaard held that the Bible is a book with our personal address on it. Certainly this message from the Second Book of Chronicles is intended for those of us who belong to the society of Jesus. It is clearly directed to the Church. 'If My people, which are called by My name. . . .' That is doubly definite. God is not here arraigning the world at large. He is pinpointing His own called-out congregation. He is naming those who name Him. Revival, like charity, begins at home. God only blesses the world through His Church. Professor Charles G. Finney, who wrote so prolifically on this subject, defined revival as the 'renewal of the first love of Christians, resulting in the conversion of sinners to God. It presupposes that the Church is backslidden, and revival means conviction of sin and searching of hearts among God's people.' Revival, then, is initially a work of the

Spirit in the Church, although the results will spill over into the world and affect it most powerfully. The first Pentecost is a pattern for all subsequent awakenings.

Perhaps the most significant word in this entire verse is the opening conjunction 'if'. It informs us that what follows lays down the conditions of revival. As Finney insists, revival is not a miracle in the sense that it appears altogether out of the blue and is wholly supernatural in its manner. It is rather 'the result of the right use of appropriate means.' Perhaps Finney went too far in reducing revival to the natural level but he was surely right to remind us that before the gift can be granted the terms must be met. God does not confer this blessing upon a vacuum. He waits until His people have prepared themselves to receive it. He may wait long after the pre-requisites are forthcoming that the manifestation may be seen to proceed from Himself and not from men. But the bestowment can never be made until the conditions have been met, even if only by a remnant within the body of believers.

Now if it is true—and God's Word assures us that it is—that revival is conditional, then it behoves us who are God's people to enquire most earnestly as to what those conditions are. This ought to be priority Number One in the Church today. The mighty revival which swept through Korea and China in 1906 and 1907 began when Jonathan Goforth made this his determination. He had stumbled on a statement by Finney that it is useless for Christians to expect revival simply by asking for it, without bothering to fulfil the laws which govern spiritual blessing. When Goforth read those words, he said: 'If Finney is right, then I am going to find out what these laws are and obey them, no matter what it costs.' That is the sort of resolution which every believer ought to make. Revival will only come when we desire it sufficiently and are ready to do all that God commands to pave the way for it. 'Blessed are they which do hunger and thirst after righteousness; for they shall be filled' (Matthew 5. 6).

This verse before us now contains the answer to such an enquiry. It lists the conditions of spiritual replenishment. As J. A. Broadbelt of Cliff College once said, it supplies 'the infallible recipe for revival'. Notice that there are four things that we must do, as the people of God called by His name, followed by three things that God will do. In this Scriptural combination the sovereignty of God and the responsibility of man are reconciled. To deny either is to depart from the Bible norm. Let us then proceed to examine in particular the fourfold obligation of believers in the matter of revival.

First, they are to HUMBLE THEMSELVES. The greatest hindrance to revival is pride amongst God's children. This, the oldest sin of all, raises an insurmountable barrier against blessing. 'God resisteth the proud and giveth grace to the humble' (I Peter 5. 5). 'The kernel of all sin is living to ourselves,' according to Dr. Alexander Maclaren, and it is this blight of selfishness that impedes revival. Again and again throughout the Scriptures blessing is reserved for the meek and lowly in heart. When men from 'Asher and Manasseh and of Zebulon humbled themselves, and came to Jerusalem' then we read that 'the Lord hearkened to Hezekiah and healed the people' (2 Chronicles 30. 11, 20). When King Josiah enquired of the Lord through Huldah, the prophetess, this was the gracious reply: 'Because thine heart was tender, and thou didst humble thyself before God, when thou heardest His words against this place, and against the inhabitants thereof, and humbledst thyself before Me, and didst rend thy clothes, and weep before Me; I have even heard thee also, saith the Lord' (2 Chronicles 34. 27).

God consistently fulfils His promise 'to revive the spirit of the humble, and to revive the heart of the contrite ones' (Isaiah 57. 15).

The great revivals of history have begun with the prostration of God's people before His face in dust and ashes. The General Assembly of the Church of Scotland in the year 1596 was specifically convened so that the ministers and commissioners might 'humble themselves and wrestle with God'. After John Davidson, that godly man, had shown from Ezekiel, in chapters Three and Thirty-Four, that faithless watchmen are accountable to God, he urged the company to make confession of sin and enter into a new covenant and league with the Lord, that by their own repentance they might the more effectively call upon others to do the same. What ensued is graphically reported by Fleming in his *Fulfilling of the Scriptures*. 'He was followed with that power for moving of their spirits in application, that within an hour after they were entered into the church, they looked with another countenance than that wherewith they entered. He exhorted them to retired meditation, and acknowledgement of their sins, even whilst they were together. For the space of a quarter of an hour they were thus humbling themselves—the preacher pausing it would seem during that time—yea, with such a joint concurrence with those sighs and groans, and with shedding of tears amongst the most, everyone provoking another by their example, and the teacher himself by his, so as the very church resounded, and that place might worthily be called a Bochim, for the like of that day had not been seen in Scotland since the Reformation.'

If God's people are eager for revival today they will humble themselves under the mighty hand of God that He may exalt them in due time. The road to blessing, whether personal or communal, runs through the needle's eye gate of lowliness. What Charles Wesley calls 'genuine, meek humility' is the first condition of renewal.

Then, again, believers are to PRAY. That is the second obligation. 'No prayer, no blessing' is an inflexible rule in all things spiritual. It is never more strongly substantiated than in revival. Prayer is the *sine qua non* of the Spirit's outflowing. Our heavenly Father will assuredly 'give the Holy Spirit to them that ask Him' (Luke 11. 13), but they must *ask*. 'Prayer, unceasing and earnest,' insisted William Burns of Kilsyth, 'is that wherein the great strength of a revival of religion lieth.' Scripture bears continuous testimony to this essential prelude to revival, from the days of Enos, then men began 'to call upon the name of the Lord' (Genesis 4. 26) down to the period prior to Pentecost when the apostles 'all continued with one accord in prayer and supplication, with the women, and Mary the mother of Jesus, and with His brethren' (Acts 1. 14), waiting for the promise of the Father. One instance out of the many will suffice to illustrate the necessity of prayer to revival. A careful scrutiny of the Book of Judges will yield the evidence for no less than five seasons of awakening. And in every case we read that beforehand 'the children of Israel cried unto the Lord.' Each time the prayer succeeds a lengthy period of oppression. The same sort of circumstances surround it. The Israelites forsake the Lord and serve the gods of other nations. Then they find themselves in bondage and at last repent and cry to God. Each time He hears their plea and sends them a saviour. Here is the impressive catalogue of answered prayer. 'The children of Israel served Chushan-rishathaim eight years. And when the children of Israel cried unto the Lord, the Lord raised up a deliverer to the children of Israel, who delivered them, even Othniel the son of Kenaz' (Judges 3. 8, 9). 'So the children of Israel served Eglon the king of Moab eighteen years. But when the children of Israel cried unto the Lord, the Lord raised them up a deliverer, Ehud the son of Gera' (4. 14, 15). 'And the Lord sold them into the hands of Jabin king of Canaan, that reigned in Hazor. . . . And the children of Israel cried unto the Lord' (5. 2, 3) and He subdued Jabin by the instrumentality of Deborah and Barak. 'And the children of Israel did evil in the sight of the Lord: and the Lord delivered them into the hand of Midian seven years. . . . And it came to pass, when the children of Israel cried unto the Lord because of the Midianites that the Lord sent a prophet unto the children of Israel' (6. 1. 7, 8) and Gideon. 'And the children of Israel did evil again in the sight of the Lord . . . and the anger of the Lord was hot against Israel, and He sold them into the hands of the Philistines, and into the hands of the children of Ammon. . . . And the children of Israel cried unto the Lord' (10. 6, 7, 10) and His answer was Jepthah.

The records of revival throughout the Christian centuries unite to testify that prevailing prayer has always preceded the recurrence of Pentecost. When God's people cast themselves upon His mercy, He opens His hand in blessing. If we do our part, He does His. Dr. R. A. Torrey used to talk about 'praying through,' and he would compare it to boring a tunnel. We start boring on our side and God starts on His. When the importunate prayer of faith and the infinite love of God have won through, the channel is clear for the power of Pentecost to work.

Further, believers are to SEEK GOD'S FACE. That is the outcome of praying through. It brings us to the unclouded presence of God. Then the light of His countenance is lifted upon us and we taste His peace. But such intimate communion with the Father is not achieved without effort. It has to be sought. God is 'a rewarder of them that diligently seek Him' (Hebrews 11. 6). He says: 'Seek ye My face' and we must respond, 'Thy face, Lord, will I seek' (Psalm 27. 8).

One of the most remarkable revivals of religion took place in the fifteenth year of Asa's reign over Judah. It is distinguished from other awakenings in that it followed a reformation. It was not a reaction from a period of apostasy but the fruition of a season of returning to the Lord. It proceeded, moreover, from an era of prosperity after national deliverance. The secret of this unusual revival is revealed in 2 Chronicles 15. 12-15. 'And they entered into a covenant to seek the Lord God of their fathers with all their heart and with all their soul; that whosoever would not seek the Lord God of Israel should be put to death, whether small or great, whether man or woman. And they sware unto the Lord with a loud voice, and with shouting, and with trumpets, and with cornets. And all Judah rejoiced at the oath; for they had sworn with all their heart, and sought Him with their whole desire; and He was found of them; and the Lord gave them rest round about.'

God is ever ready to be entreated. He longs for His children to seek His face and live. He intends His Church to enjoy the beatitude of abundance. 'For I know the thoughts that I think toward you, saith the Lord, thoughts of peace, and not of evil, to give you an expected end (or, a future and a hope). Then shall ye call upon Me, and ye shall go and pray unto Me, and I will hearken unto you. And ye shall seek Me, and find Me, when ye shall search for Me with all your heart' (Jeremiah 29. 11-13).

Finally, believers are to TURN FROM SIN. It is an ineluctable condition of revival that God's people should forsake their wicked ways. There must be a burning of all boats and a clean-cut break with every known iniquity. No Achan must remain unrebuked and unrepentant in the camp or Ai will not fall. This is the sternest requirement for revival. It calls for the surgeon's knife, but without it there can be no spiritual recovery.

It has been said that the Seventh Chapter in the Book of Joshua is the greatest lesson on revival in the whole of Scripture. It will repay an unhurried re-reading with the help of the Interpreter Spirit. Like Israel of old, the Church today has been defeated at Ai and halts on the borders of the Promised Land. The godly remnant echoes the plaintive prayer of Joshua: 'O Lord, what shall I say, when Israel turneth their backs before their enemies! For the Canaanites and all the inhabitants of the land shall hear of it, and shall environ us round, and cut off our name from the earth: and what wilt Thou do unto Thy great name?' (Joshua 7. 8, 9). It is God's honour that is at stake as well as ours. And still the answer comes to us as it came to Joshua those many years ago. 'Israel hath sinned, and they have also transgressed My covenant which I commanded them: for they have even taken of the accursed thing' (v. 11). No victory can be expected whilst sin is unconfessed. Repentance must needs precede revival. God cannot do His mighty works whilst wickedness prevails within. 'Neither will I be with you any more, except ye destroy the accursed from among you' (v. 12). And only when the offence is removed can the battle be won.

That is how it must always be. Unless God's people are prepared to turn from their wicked ways the door to revival is closed. Let this then be the cry of every soul: 'Search me, O God, and know my heart; try me, and know my thoughts: and see if there be any wicked way in me' (Psalm 139. 23, 24). And let us recall that the sin of omission is just as heinous in God's sight as the sin of commission. It is not enough to say that we have done no evil, however improbable even that may be. If we have failed to do all the good we might, we fall under equal condemnation. That we have not prayed as long or as often as God calls us to do: that we have not served His cause and Kingdom with the zeal He requires: that we have not sought to lead others to the Lord with the earnestness He demands—this is the measure of our iniquity. Remember that sin means missing the mark. 'All unrighteousness is sin' (1 John 5. 17)—all that comes short of the glory of God. 'Thou wicked and slothful servant' was the rebuke reserved for the man who hid his talent in the earth (Matthew 25. 26): we might even say 'wicked *because* slothful.'

Yet, with all their penitence and godly sorrow for sin, the people of God can only turn from their wicked ways as He Himself gently constrains them. 'Turn us, O God of our salvation, and cause Thine anger towards us to cease' (Psalm 85. 4). It was such a realisation that ushered in the Moravian revival. Young Count Nicholas Zinzendorf pondered long the dying petition of Jan Amos Comenius, a Bishop of the Bohemian Brethren. 'I could not peruse the lamentations of old Comenius addressed to the Anglican Church—lamentations called forth by the idea that the Church of the Brethren was coming to an end, and that he was locking its door. I could not read his mournful prayer, "Turn Thou us unto Thee, O Lord, and we shall be turned; renew our days as of old" (Lamentations 5. 21), without resolving there and then: "I will, as far as I can, help to bring about this renewal".' God mightily honoured that penitential resolution and the rejuvenation of Moravianism spread attendant blessings far and wide, not least in the spiritual enlightenment of John Wesley which heralded the Evangelical Awakening here in Britain.

These, then, are the conditions of revival as prescribed by the Word of God. His children must humble themselves, and pray, and seek His face and turn from sin. Then, He infallibly promises, 'will I hear from heaven, and will forgive their sin, and will heal their land.' When men meet God's conditions, God meets their needs. Delay is due to our unwillingness, not to His reluctance. 'Behold, the Lord's hand is not shortened, that it cannot save; neither His ear heavy, that it cannot hear: but your iniquities have separated between you and your God, and your sins have hid His face from you, that He will not hear' (Isaiah 59. 1, 2). As Sidlow Baxter has written with reference to this red-letter verse from 2 Chronicles 7. 14, 'God's heart is not hardened against us. He waits to be gracious, and to renew His former mercies. His arms are wide to receive us. His heart melts with compassion. He yearns over His sinning, erring, suffering, human children. If My people. . . . O God, bring Thine own people to the place of heart-searching and imploring prayer: Bless Thy people. Save our land. Glorify Thy name.'

CHAPTER IV

THE NATURE OF REVIVAL

'Drop down, ye heavens, from above, and let the skies pour down righteousness: let the earth open, and let them bring forth salvation, and let righteousness spring up together; I the Lord have created it.' —Isaiah 45. 8

THE definitions of revival are legion. Every book on the subject has supplied its own. But there is unity in this diversity. The many attempts to crystallize the meaning of revival in a single statement represent variations on a theme. There are no serious discrepancies. It is simply that revival is a many-splendoured thing and can no more be confined to a formula than the grace of God.

According to the Oxford Dictionary, revival in the specifically Christian sense of the term, means the 'reawakening of religious fervour.' John Bonar described it as 'the exchange of the form of godliness for its living power—the coming of life where life has never been, notwithstanding the long and fond profession of it.' He amplified his account by adding that, viewed with respect to the Church, revival is a time of newness of life, and reviewed in respect to the world it is a time of multiplied conversions. In the language of Calvin Colton, one of the earliest writers on American revivals, it is 'the multiplied power of religion over a community of minds, when the Spirit of God awakens Christians to special faith and effort, and brings sinners to repentance.' 'New life bringing a new joy—that is a fair description of a revival of religion,' declared Dr. John S. Simon, the Methodist historian, on the basis of Psalm 85. 6. 'The experiences of the day of Pentecost repeat themselves,' he continued, 'and the weary Church finding its lost youth, walks in the morning light of Apostolic days.' 'A revival breaks the power of the world and of sin over Christians', wrote Finney. 'It brings them to such vantage ground that they get a fresh impulse toward heaven; they have a new foretaste of heaven, and new desires after union with God; and the charm of the world is broken, and the power of sin overcome.' 'A revival is a voluntary and determined return to first things,' said Principal John D. Drysdale, 'and a whole-hearted honouring of God as Creator, Jesus Christ as our Lord and Saviour, and the Holy Ghost as our Sanctifier.' And to round off this selection, here is D. M. Panton: 'Revival is (as at Pentecost) the localized presence of Deity, revealing man to himself, and so shaking the soul to its foundations.' These, then, are just a few of the manifold definitions of revival. Each of them throws light upon some aspect that otherwise might have been overlooked.

But of course the best and surest guide to the nature of revival is Scripture itself. Here we learn all we need to know on every topic that is essential to Gospel truth, and here therefore we shall expect to discover the fundamental significance of revival. Few of the standard Bible dictionaries do justice to the importance of such an enquiry and there is real need for thorough linguistic research in this field. Within the limits of this present essay we can do no more than mark out the terrain. It is the Old Testament that provides us with the bulk of our relevant material. Revival is throughout associated with varying forms of the root *hāyā*, to live. The general sense of the verb usually (though not uniformly) translated 'to revive' is to quicken, to impart fresh life. That is the implication, for instance, of Ecclesiastes 7. 12. 'The excellence of knowledge is, that wisdom *giveth life* to them that have it.' In Hosea 14. 7 it is used with reference to grain, and 'they shall *revive* as the corn' might be rendered 'be caused to grow.' In 1 Chronicles 11. 8 we read 'And Joab *repaired* the rest of the city': that affords us with another and pregnant connotation of revival, for the root is the same (cf. Nehemiah 4. 2).

A whole series of usages suggest the idea of recovery or restoration. It may be from discouragement, as in Genesis 45. 27 where 'when he saw the wagons which Joseph had sent to carry him, the spirit of Jacob their father *revived*.' It may be from exhaustion, as in Judges 15. 19 where Samson, after slaying a thousand men with the jaw-bone of an ass, was sore athirst, 'but God clave an hollow place that was in the jaw, and there came water thereout; and when he had drunk, his spirit came again, and he *revived*.' It may be from slavery, as in Ezra 9. 8 where the priest of the restoration gave thanks to God for granting 'a little *reviving*' in their bondage. Often the recovery referred to is from sickness and disease. When the children of Israel had been plagued with fiery serpents in the wilderness, Moses, we are told, made a brazen likeness of the offending creature and lifted it up before the people. 'And it came to pass, that if a serpent had bitten any man, when he beheld the serpent of brass, he *lived*' (Numbers 21. 9), or, rather, lived again, that is, revived. A derivative from the same verb is employed in Ahazia's enquiry concerning his recovery (2 Kings 1. 2), the story of Naaman's cleansing from leprosy (2 Kings 5. 7), and the prophecy of Elisha about Benhadad's restoration (2 Kings 8. 10).

On many occasions forms of this selfsame root appear in passages which relate to resuscitation from physical death. This is the distinctive prerogative of the living God. He alone gives life and He alone restores life. 'The Lord killeth and maketh alive; He bringeth down to the grave, and bringeth up' (1 Samuel 2. 6). In this sense cognates of the verb 'to revive' are used to describe the restoration of the Shunammite's son and of the man buried in the sepulchre of Elisha (2 Kings 8. 5 and 13. 21). In the case of the widow's child at Zarephath, revival occurred when 'the soul came into him again' (1 Kings 17. 22); in the case of the resurrection of dry bones in Ezekiel 37 revival occurred when 'the breath came into them' (v. 10). The word is found with similar meaning in Hosea 6. 2: 'After two days will He *revive* us: in the third day He will raise us up, and we shall live in His sight,' no doubt with a veiled Messianic implication. Two other instances clearly fall into this category. The first is an enquiry about personal survival: 'If a man die, shall he *live again?*' (Job 14. 14). The second anticipates the general resurrection: 'Thy dead men shall *live*, together with my dead body shall they rise. Awake and sing, ye that dwell in dust: for thy dew is as the dew of herbs, and the earth shall cast out the dead' (Isaiah 26. 19).

We are now left with a set of occurrences in the Book of Psalms where this same verb takes on a special tone with reference to spiritual revival, either individual or communal. The note in the Brown, Driver and Briggs Hebrew-English Lexicon on this technical signification is most instructive: 'to revive the people of Jehovah, by Jehovah Himself, with fulness of life in His favour.' The first time the Psalmist resorts to this term there is an obvious link with the last class listed above. 'Thou, which hast shewed me great and sore troubles, shalt *quicken* me again, and shalt bring me up again from the depths of the earth' (Psalm 71. 20). Psalm 80. 18, 19 is obviously relevant to the revival of God's people as we understand it nowadays: 'So will not we go back from Thee: *quicken* us, and we will call upon Thy name. Turn us again, O Lord God of hosts, cause Thy face to shine:

and we shall be saved.' Passing over the familiar 6th verse of Psalm 85, which will form the text of a later chapter, we reach the 119th Psalm which positively teems with examples. 'To quicken' recurs no less than eleven times. In each case the revival involved is personal. Nine times over the Psalmist prays 'Quicken Thou me.' In v. 25 it is 'Quicken Thou me according to Thy Word.' In v. 37 'Quicken Thou me in Thy way.' In v. 40 'Quicken me in Thy righteousness.' In v. 88 'Quicken me after Thy loving kindness.' In v. 107 again 'Quicken me, O Lord, according to Thy Word.' In v. 149 'Quicken me according to Thy judgment.' In v. 154 yet again 'Quicken me according to Thy Word.' In v. 156 'Quicken me according to Thy judgments.' And in v. 159 'Quicken me according to Thy loving-kindness.' Twice the Psalmist testifies that God has already revived him. 'This is my comfort in my affliction, for Thy Word hath quickened me' (v. 50): 'I will never forget Thy precepts: for with them Thou hast quickened me' (v. 93). This repeated plea for personal revival which runs like a refrain throughout the exceptional length of the 119th Psalm brings a challenge to every believer. It points to the only way of blessing. Before we pray 'Revive us, O Lord,' each one of us must be ready to ask 'Revive *me*, O Lord.' Again with the Psalmist, we must make this our petition: 'Teach *me* to do Thy will; for Thou art *my* God: Thy Spirit is good; lead Me into the land of uprightness. Quicken *me*, O Lord, for Thy name's sake' (Psalm 143. 10, 11).

A memorable tale is told of those two great stalwarts of God, Dr. F. B. Meyer and Dr. G. Campbell Morgan. They had travelled together to Cardiff in the early days of the Welsh revival of 1904. A fine upstanding policeman was on traffic control duty outside the railway station, so the Doctors of Divinity approached him to ask where the revival was. He put his hand on his heart and with a radiant face he replied, 'Gentlemen, it is here.' That is where revival is to be found. It is no abstraction. God does not waste His matchless energy in vitalising empty space and thin air. His work is done in people: first in His own people and then through them in His lost people. Revival is a quickening of hearts and unless it begins in yours and mine it will never spread.

In the period between the two world wars the Christian Church in China inaugurated a Five Year Plan for advancement. The motto commended to every member was this: 'Lord, revive Thy Church, beginning from me.' That is where revival must always start. The foregoing survey of Old Testament vocabulary has brought us to a sharp realisation of that fact. May we sing the old chorus with a new sincerity:

> 'Lord, send a revival
> And let it begin in me.'

A similar word study in the New Testament would be equally valuable and instructive. Although the Authorised Version only translates two Greek verbs appearing in three places as 'to revive' the frequency is greater than might be supposed. The word which is used in Romans 7. 9 to describe the revival of sin in face of the commandment, and in Romans 14. 9 with reference to our Lord's return to life from the grave, is also employed in Luke 15. 24 where the father of the prodigal announces, 'For this my son was dead and *is alive again.*' The other verb occurs only in Philippians 4. 10 and is originally a gardening term which alludes to the blooming of flowers in springtime.

But if we had time to embark upon an exhaustive examination of the vocabulary of revival in the Scriptures of the New Testament we should have to notice also the numerous instances where the verb rendered 'to quicken' is found in the sacred text. The reader who will consult those passages with a concordance as his guide will be richly repaid. And indeed the entire terminology of the Spirit would have to be surveyed if we were to obtain a comprehensive picture of what the New Testament teaches about the nature of revival. Much of it, however, will be dealt with in further chapters of this book, so we can close the investigation for the present at this point.

We shall now turn to the verse from Isaiah 45 which lies open before us. 'Drop down, ye heavens, from above, and let the skies pour down righteousness: let the earth open, and let them bring forth salvation, and let righteousness spring up together; I the Lord have created it.' This beautiful passage from the Old Testament Scriptures came by inspiration to one who longed and interceded for revival. Here we have the God-breathed language of one who vehemently desired an increase of genuine piety and who was accustomed to look forward to times of refreshing from the hand of the Lord. Isaiah has been rightly denominated the evangelical prophet and he, more than any other, delighted to describe the shower of Gospel blessing associated with an awakening of the Spirit. Professor O. C. Whitehouse has aptly characterised this fervent outburst as a lyrical effusion or intermezzo. Our hearts thrill to the music of the celestial spheres as we rehearse it. It is all the more surprising and remarkable in that it is included in the charge to Cyrus, the Persian ruler, who is nevertheless the instrument of God's sovereign and mysterious purpose.

This little-studied verse reveals something more concerning the nature of revival. It tells us, first WHENCE REVIVAL COMES. 'Drop down, ye heavens, from above, and let the skies pour down righteousness.' 'Drop down' . . . 'from above' . . . 'pour down'—these phrases of the

Word disclose the source of revival. Like every good and perfect gift, it 'is from above, and cometh down from the Father of lights, with whom there is no variableness, neither shadow of turning' (James 1. 17). Revival is a supernatural phenomenon and it has a supernatural origin. It is a gift from God. Being the outpouring of God's everlasting mercy, 'it droppeth as the gentle rain from heaven upon the place beneath.'

Revival is not the manufacture of man. No human agency can bring it about. As Ernest Baker has said, 'a revival cannot be organised any more than the spring.' It is from above and nothing from below can contribute to it. It is not an earthly concoction: it is a heavenly creation. 'There is scarcely anything we have the handling of,' observed Richard Baxter, 'but we leave on it the prints of our fingers.' Revival is unmarked by any such defilement. It is untouched by hand. It is all God's own work. Again and again the records of revival testify to its Divine origin. Here is Bishop Handley Moule recalling his impressions of the Dorset awakening in which both he and Evan Hopkins were converted. 'I must not close without a memory, however meagre, of one wonderful epoch in the parish. It was the Revival. The year was 1859, that "year of the right hand of the Most High. . . ." Ulster was profoundly and lastingly moved and blessed. Here and there in England it was the same: and Fordington was one of the scenes of Divine Awakening. For surely it was Divine. No artificial means of excitement were dreamt of; my father's whole genius was against it. No powerful personality, no Moody or Aitken, came to us. A city missionary and a London Bible-woman were the only helpers from a distance. But a power not of man brought souls to ask the old question: "What must I do to be saved"?'

That is the nature of revival blessing. It comes from

the hand of the Lord to bring renewal to the face of the earth. It fulfils the Scripture promise: 'He shall come down like rain upon the mown grass: as showers that water the earth' (Psalm 72. 6).

This verse also tells us How REVIVAL IS RECEIVED. 'Let the earth open.' It is as simple as that. Just as the parched ground lays itself bare to the gift of rain, so God's people are to wait for the shower of blessing. They are, as we have seen, to humble themselves, and pray and seek God's face and turn from sin. They are to spend and be spent in winning souls and ministering to the necessities not only of the saints, but also of all who have been left bruised and broken on the Jericho road of life. But in respect of revival, when we have done all we are still unprofitable servants and can never hope to earn revival as a reward for faithfulness. One word contains the secret—'let the earth *open.*'

How hard it is for us to accept revival as a bestowal from God's bounty! The fallacy of works invades even our conception of spiritual quickening. We want to feel that we have done something towards it. We tend to imagine that God is helpless without our efforts. And so we are continually driving ourselves and our fellow-believers to greater endeavours. It is good that we should be always abounding in the work of the Lord, but we should remember that the work is indeed His and not ours, and that no amount of zeal on our part, however determined and even frenzied, can in itself effect a revival. It is not what we do for God but what He does for us that constitutes revival.

Early in the Welsh awakening of 1904 a Wiltshire evangelist visited the meetings at Ferndale. He stood up and said, 'Friends, I have journeyed into Wales with the hope that I may glean the secret of the Welsh Revival.' In an instant, Evan Roberts was on his feet, and with an uplifted arm towards the speaker, he replied: 'My brother, there is no secret. Ask and ye shall receive.' That is how revival comes. 'Ye have not, because ye ask not. Ye ask, and receive not, because ye ask amiss' (James 4. 2, 3).

This verse further tells us WHAT REVIVAL PRODUCES. 'Let them bring forth salvation, and let righteousness spring up together.' These are the twin end-products of revival. Salvation, of course, is the grand object of every time of refreshing. God quickens that He may save. God, 'Who will have all men to be saved, and to come unto the knowledge of the truth' (1 Timothy 2. 4), prepares these seasons of renewal for the purpose of salvation. God doth not 'respect any person, yet doth He devise means, that His banished be not expelled from Him' (2 Samuel 14. 14). That was the salient feature of Pentecost. 'And the Lord added to the church daily such as should be saved' (Acts 2. 47).

The second product of revival is righteousness. This is a different word in the Hebrew from that used earlier in the verse. That which comes down from heaven is *tsedeq*; that which springs from the earth is *tsedaqah*. The first is cause and the second is effect. The former is the Divine endowment and the latter is its outworking on the human plane. Salvation necessarily issues in righteousness. When a man is put right with God he will soon be right with his fellows as well. His entire way of life will be affected. Any spiritual experience which does not evidence itself in such moral realignment is rightly suspect. Paul's prayer for his Philippian converts is appropriate to every newborn soul. 'That ye may approve the things that are excellent; that ye may be sincere and without offence till the day of Christ; being filled with the fruits of righteousness, which are by Jesus Christ, unto the glory and praise of God' (Philippians 1. 10, 11). Here is the very essence of righteousness.

This, then, is the nature of revival. It comes from above. It is received by the openness of faith. It produces salvation and righteousness. And before this verse from Isaiah 45 reaches its end, God sets His own seal to the work. 'I the Lord have created it,' He says. That is the Maker's mark stamped indelibly upon the product. And as the gift is His, so its aim is that He may have all the glory. The final objective of revival is to magnify the majesty and mercy of our incomparable Redeemer. 'I am the Lord, and there is none else, there is no God beside Me: I girded thee, though thou hast not known Me: that they may know from the rising of the sun, and from the west, that there is none beside Me. I am the Lord, and there is none else' (Isaiah 45. 5, 6).

CHAPTER V

THE PRICE OF REVIVAL

'And Samuel spake unto all the house of Israel, saying,
If ye do return unto the Lord with all your hearts, then put
away the strange gods and Ashtaroth from among you, and
prepare your hearts unto the Lord, and serve Him only: and
He will deliver you out of the hand of the Philistines.'

I Samuel 7. 3

THE passage to which we next devote our attention relates to an outstanding outbreak of revival. It is one of the highlights of the Old Testament Scriptures in this respect. 'Few words are here used,' remarks an old commentator, 'but they are so expressive that we cannot hesitate to pronounce this one of the most general and effectual revivals of religion which ever took place in the Church of Israel.' We cannot therefore afford to overlook the lessons of this exceptional manifestation of the Spirit's intervention. They have to do with the price that is to be paid for revival. Quickening is always a costly thing. It cannot, of course, be bought, but it is never cheaply obtained. It is the free bestowal of God and yet it has to be preceded by the sacrifice of His people. There, indeed, lies the paradox of revival.

The circumstances into which this awakening irrupted are deeply instructive and even encouraging to those who despair of any sort of renascence of things spiritual. A dark page in Israel's history was just concluding. Both the religious and national life of God's chosen heritage was at a perilously low ebb. For twenty years they had languished in dire adversity. They had been beaten in battle at Ebenezer by the Philistine enemy and now they were reduced to abject serfdom. They suffered all the privation and ignominy of an occupied land. Their lives were scarcely their own. Meanwhile, the worship of Jehovah had virtually ceased. It had seriously declined even before the military catastrophe. Eli had allowed his profligate and greedy sons to usurp the sacred authority of the priesthood and to abuse it for their own iniquitous ends. Not surprisingly, the people had fallen into indifference if not into actual apostasy. Then came the Philistine invasion to administer a stunning blow to the external expression of religion in the regular ritual of worship. The ark of God, which had degenerated into a superstitious symbol, was captured by the foe, and borne in triumph into the temple of Dagon in Ashdod. The priestly house was exterminated. The national shrine at Shiloh was devastated and the faithful few had no recognised place of assembly. Eventually the ark proved too uncomfortable a trophy for the Philistines and was returned to Israel, where it lay in the residence of Abinadab in Kirjath-jearim. Such was the condition of the nation on the eve of revival. The outlook could hardly have been less propitious. Yet it was in a midnight hour like this that the Lord was about to bless His people. Of a truth, man's extremity is God's opportunity.

But first the price had to be paid. The stirrings of repentance can be discerned in verse 2. 'And it came to pass, while the ark abode in Kirjath-jearim, that the time was long; for it was twenty years; and all the house of Israel lamented after the Lord.' 'Lost blessings are precious', comments Alexander Maclaren. 'God was more prized when withdrawn.' At long last His chosen began to yearn for Him again. There was an aching void within that the world could never fill. The broken cisterns had failed as they always do. They lamented after the Lord— 'as a child follows the father who has been forced to turn away in anger,' says Professor G. D. Kirkpatrick, 'and with sighs and tears entreats for reconciliation.'

At this moment of incipient penitence, the prophet Samuel dramatically reappears on the scene. We read in 1 Samuel 4. 1 that 'the word of Samuel came to all Israel.' No more is heard of him until this Seventh Chapter. There is no mention of him in the account of Israel's defeat at Ebenezer or throughout the long years of tyranny. God had hidden His face because of sin, and His messenger was silenced. But as soon as Israel begins to think once more upon the Lord, Samuel returns. Once again he addresses all the house of Israel. He tells them what they must do if they are truly sincere in their desire to seek the Lord. He reminds them of the costliness that attaches to spiritual quickening. He asks in effect whether they are ready to pay the price.

There is an intended contrast between the inadequate preparations before the first fight at Ebenezer and these which precede the second engagement on the same spot. On that previous and tragic occasion, all they had done was to carry the ark into the camp as if it were a magic charm to ward off danger. Their religion had been reduced to little more than heathen idolatry and the holy object was treated simply as a fetish. In a period of spiritual declension a similar tendency invariably impoverishes the worship of God. Nominal believers rely upon the outward sign rather than the inward reality of Christian faith. They suppose that ecclesiastical ordinances or sacramental rites can of themselves ensure spiritual vitality. And such virtual idolatry spells ultimate doom. A swift nemesis descends upon those who change the truth of God into a lie and worship and serve the creature more than the Creator (cf. Romans 1. 25).

How different is the attitude and approach recommended here by Samuel prior to the second engagement with the Philistine foe at Ebenezer! Already the house of Israel has lamented after the Lord and now the prophet points the way to victory. If they do indeed intend to return to Jehovah and be His children once again, then they must be prepared to meet the cost involved. For revival is not without its price.

We learn from this verse that the price of revival includes THE PRICE OF HOLINESS, which is separation from the world. God's people have to turn away from evil. 'If ye do return unto the Lord with all your hearts, then put away the strange gods and Ashtaroth from among you.' These idols were the male and female deities of the Babylonian religion imported into the land of Canaan by the pagan community. So far had the Israelites fallen from the pure worship of Jehovah that they too had bowed down to such images of wood and stone. Before ever God can revive His faithless people they must first forsake their false gods. 'Thou shalt have no other gods before Me,' demands the Lord. 'Thou shalt not make unto thee any graven image, or any likeness of any thing that is in heaven above, or that is in the earth beneath, or that is in the water under the earth. Thou shalt not bow down thyself to them, nor serve them: for I the Lord Thy God am a jealous God' (Exodus 20. 3-5). Revival requires a break with every cherished sin within the congregation of His flock. Israel must abandon even the dearest idol it has known.

The Word of God is inescapably unambiguous on this issue. 'Ye adulterers and adulteresses, know ye not that the friendship of the world is enmity with God? whosoever therefore will be a friend of the world is the enemy of God' (James 4. 4). 'If ye were of the world, the world would love his own,' said our Lord, 'but because ye are not of the world, but I have chosen you out of the world, therefore the world hateth you' (John 15. 19). Christ has no part with Belial, neither he who believes with an infidel. The temple of God has no agreement with idols. 'Wherefore come out from among them, and be ye separate, saith the Lord, and touch not any unclean thing; and I will receive you, and I will be a Father unto you, and ye shall be My sons and daughters, saith the Lord God Almighty' (2 Corinthians 6. 17, 18).

The question of worldliness is one of the most crucial tests of the Christian Church today. If we fail here we may forfeit blessing for generations to come. 'For the time is come that judgment must begin at the house of God' (1 Peter 4. 17). We tend to blame circumstances for the present ineptitude of organised Christianity. We should rather enquire within. We must ask whether we have indeed put away the strange gods and Ashtaroth from among us. Is it not sadly true that world is too much with us? We are suffering from the infiltration of secular standards and motives within the society of the saved. We hear much today, and rightly so, about the need for the Church to move out into the world in evangelism. But the Church can only effectively venture into the world when the world has been driven out of the Church. That is the challenge of the present hour.

The mighty revival under Asa began when he 'took courage, and put away the abominable idols out of all the land of Judah and Benjamin, and out of the cities which he had taken from mount Ephraim, and renewed the altar of the Lord, that was before the porch of the Lord' (2 Chronicles 15. 8). The similar awakening in the reign of Hezekiah can be traced to the day when 'they gathered their brethren, and sanctified themselves, and came, according to the commandment of the king, by the words of the Lord, to cleanse the house of the Lord. And the priests went into the inner part of the house of the Lord, to cleanse it, and brought out all the uncleanness that they found in the temple of the Lord into the court of the house of the Lord. And the Levites took, it to carry it out abroad into the brook Kidron' (2 Chronicles 29. 15, 16). The same separation preceded the reformation under Josiah, for we read: 'And Josiah took away all the abominations out of all the countries that pertained to the children of Israel, and made all that were present in Israel to serve, even to serve the Lord their God' (2 Chronicles 34. 33).

We stand in desperate need of such drastic cleansing within the Church today. All our machinery and ritual is of no avail unless we put away the evil of our doings from before the eyes of the Lord. God is not pleased with the multitude of sacrifices unless there is a genuine forsaking of sin (cf. Isaiah 1. 11-20). There can be no policy of co-existence with worldliness. As Nehemiah recognised, the first step to revival is to rebuild the wall. The line of demarcation has to be re-established between the Church and the world around. Only a holy assembly can be used by God to bring healing to mankind. 'And I will sanctify My great name, which was profaned among the heathen, which ye have profaned in the midst of them; and the heathen shall know that I am the Lord, saith the Lord God, when I shall be sanctified in you before their eyes' (Ezekiel 36. 23). Holiness is essential to revival. 'Till you press believers to expect full salvation now,' wrote John Wesley to George Merryweather, in 1766, 'you must not look for any revival.'

The price of revival includes THE PRICE OF STEADFAST-NESS, which is reliance upon God. God's people have to lean hard on Him. 'If ye do return unto the Lord with all your hearts, then . . . prepare your hearts unto the Lord.' Moffatt has 'set your hearts on the Eternal' and the Revised Standard Version Bible renders 'direct your hearts to the Lord.' The verb suggests the ideas of reorientation and establishment. God's people are to turn from their idols and look to the Lord: they are to stop trusting in the creature and rely upon the Creator.

That is perhaps the costliest element in revival. It is hard to abandon our own self-sufficiency and rest in the Lord. We prefer to do our own thinking and planning, even if afterwards we belatedly apply to God for approval. But to prepare our hearts unto the Lord and to place all our reliance upon Him is a trial to our proud nature. Yet it is the sole secret of steadfastness. Only when the needle coincides with the north can we be sure that we shall not miss our providential way. George Matheson, the blind preacher of Scotland, put it into a searching verse.

> 'My will is not my own
>   Till Thou hast made it Thine;
> If it would reach a monarch's throne
>   It must its crown resign;
> It only stands unbent
>   Amid the clashing strife
> When on Thy bosom it has leant
>   And found in Thee its life.'

The Psalmist had entered into this necessary experience. 'My soul, wait Thou only upon God; for my expectation is from Him. He only is my rock and my salvation: He is my defence; I shall not be moved' (Psalm 62. 5, 6). And what he has discovered himself he commends to others. 'Cast thy burden upon the Lord, and He shall sustain thee: He shall never suffer the righteous to be moved' (Psalm 55. 22). 'A man shall not be established by wickedness': says the Book of Proverbs, 'but the root of the righteous shall not be moved' (Proverbs 12. 3). The same insistence on steadfastness occurs in the Scriptures of the New Testament. 'Therefore, my beloved brethren, be ye steadfast, unmoveable, always abounding in the work of the Lord, forasmuch as ye know that your labour

is not in vain in the Lord' (1 Corinthians 15. 58). In that
exhortation the apostle shows the true relationship
between trusting and toiling. We are inclined to put
work before waiting and labour before faith. God's
Word reverses the order. Our work will be of little
worth unless first we have waited on God and labour
will be lost unless it springs from faith. That is profoundly
relevant to the Church's preparation for revival. We
must first of all 'prepare our hearts unto the Lord.' We
must 'continue in the faith grounded and settled, and be
not moved away from the hope of the Gospel' (Colossians
1. 23).

Fidelity to God in the midst of a wicked and adulterous
generation such as ours will demand the highest price.
Only as we are ready to forego pleasure and popularity
and worldly advancement shall we remain steadfast
before the storm. Those who have truly prepared their
hearts unto the Lord will be moved neither by shame
nor scorn, by deprivation nor persecution. Come what
may, they will remain on the rock. The righteous shall
not be moved for ever: 'he shall not be afraid of evil
tidings: his heart is fixed, trusting in the Lord' (Psalm
112. 7). He knows that what he has to endure is part of
the birth-pangs of revival. 'Who can hurt us if God is
on our side?' asked Wesley once in a letter to Adam
Clarke. 'Trials may come, but they are all good. I have
not been so tried for many years. Every week and almost
every day I am bespattered in the public papers. Many
are in tears on the occasion; many, terribly frightened
and crying out, "Oh, what will the end be?" What will
it be? Why, glory to God in the highest, and peace and
goodwill among men.'

The price of revival includes THE PRICE OF SUBMISSIVE-
NESS, which is concentration of aim. God's people have
to bow down to Him alone. 'If ye do return unto the

Lord with all your hearts, then . . . serve Him only.' It must be Him only if it is to be Him at all. Real religion, like real love, is exclusive. 'Ye cannot serve God and mammon' (Matthew 6. 24). God's children must submit unreservedly to Him. Their life and witness will be marked by singleness of purpose. To serve Him only will be their constant aim. They will covet the submissiveness of Enoch, 'for before his translation he had this testimony, that he pleased God' (Hebrews 11. 5).

There is one title common to nearly all the great figures of Scripture through whom God has brought revival to His children. It is applied to Abraham, to Moses, to Joshua, to David, to Elijah, to Isaiah and to all the prophets in a body from Amos onwards. They are called 'servant of God' or 'servant of the Lord.' The selfsame designation is assumed by the authors of the New Testament epistles—Peter, James, Jude and repeatedly by Paul. The word is a strong one and means a bondslave. The servant is bound to his master by law and duty. He is virtually the property of his employer. That is how the great men of God have conceived their relationship with Him. They have been utterly subservient to the Lord. They have been, in the phrase of S. D. Gordon, 'the pliant instruments of His will.'

God calls all believers to be servants of His. We are to 'serve Him only.' Like the slaves of old, we are bound to one master. We are to be less than the dust before Him. Only when we are so bowed and broken at His feet can He begin to use us. Only when we submit can He control. Only when we are nothing can He be everything. Francis of Assisi was once asked how he was able to accomplish so much in the service of the Lord. 'This may be why,' he answered. 'The Lord looked down from heaven and said, "Where can I find the weakest, meanest man on earth?" Then He found me, and said, "I have found him; I will work through him. He will not be proud of it for he will know I am only using him because of his insignificance".' Submissiveness is always the secret of usefulness.

But a price has to be paid before Christians are brought thus low. We have to attend what Oswald Chambers used to call a white funeral. We have to die to self and sin in order to rise into the likeness of Christ. George Müller of Bristol was on one occasion confronted by the same enquiry as Francis faced. He was questioned about the secret of his remarkable ministry. 'There was a day,' he said, 'when I died, utterly died to George Müller, his opinions and preferences, tastes and will: died to the world, its approval or censure: died to the approval or blame even of my brethren and friends, and since then I have striven only to show myself approved unto God.' That is where revival begins.

To the price in this verse there is appended a promise. 'And He will deliver you out of the hand of the Philistines.' Victory is assured when the cost has been met. And God was as good as His word, as He always is. The Philistines were vanquished on the very site of their former triumph. 'The Lord thundered with a great thunder on that day against the Philistines, and discomfited them; and they were smitten before Israel' (v. 10). So complete was the rout that 'they came no more into the coast of Israel' (v. 13). But only because first of all the challenge of Samuel's speech was accepted. He pronounced the price the people paid it. 'Then the children of Israel did put away Baalim and Ashtaroth, and served the Lord only' (v. 4). Only when they were ready for *all* His perfect will could the blessing fall. That is still the price of revival.

CHAPTER VI

THE VERGE OF REVIVAL

'And it came to pass at the time of the offering of the evening sacrifice, that Elijah the prophet came near, and said, Lord God of Abraham, Isaac, and of Israel, let it be known this day that Thou art God in Israel, and that I am Thy servant, and that I have done all these things at Thy word. Hear me, O Lord, hear me, that this people may know that Thou art the Lord God, and that Thou hast turned their heart back again. Then the fire of the Lord fell. . . .'   —I Kings 18. 36-38

R EVIVAL cannot be reduced to a schedule. The Spirit obeys no laws but those of the Father. He enjoys a Divine liberty. It is not therefore possible to draw up a timetable of revival. It cannot be controlled by the clock. It runs its own God-directed course. When, for the purposes of exposition, we speak in this chapter and the next first about the verge of revival and then of its advent, it must not be supposed that any rigid distinctions can be drawn. We can no more say precisely where a powerful movement of the Spirit passes over into revival than we can tell exactly where a mountain stream becomes a river. In each case the one flows into the other.

The section before us from 1 Kings 18. 36-38 quite clearly refers, nevertheless, to the eleventh hour before revival breaks out. The clue lies at the beginning of verse 38: '*Then* the fire of the Lord fell,' and the response of the people, when they prostrated themselves and confessed, 'The Lord, He is the God; the Lord, He is the God' indicates that revival was under way. Without tracing any hard and fast lines beyond what the Word of God would authorise, we may yet profitably enquire as to the immediate preliminaries of revival. They are sufficiently suggested in this portion of God's Book.

Some account of the situation underlying the contest on Mount Carmel must first be supplied if we are to grasp to the full the implications of the story. The reign of Ahab over Israel exerted a sinister influence. The comment of the sacred oracles upon the twenty-two years of his rule is that he 'did evil in the sight of the Lord above all that were before him' (1 Kings 16. 30). Since this sad verdict is also passed upon his predecessor Zimri we rightly conclude that in Ahab mounting iniquity came to a head. But as if it were not enough that he emulated the sins of his fathers, he took to himself a wife from a heathen land and encouraged the worship of Baal in Israel. He erected an altar and himself served Baal and worshipped him. So it is recorded with sorrow that 'Ahab did more to provoke the Lord God of Israel to anger than all the kings of Israel that were before him' (1 Kings 16. 33).

Outwardly Ahab was to all intents and purposes a successful monarch. He promoted the public welfare in many material ways. He constructed new cities and added yet another royal residence to Israel. He fulfilled the ideal of a military leader who was not afraid to go into battle with his men and who gained considerable victories against the Syrians. Moreover, he pursued a policy of friendship with the southern kingdom of Judah and cemented the recent alliance. But 'the Lord seeth not as man seeth; for man looketh on the outward appearance, but the Lord looketh on the heart' (1 Samuel 16. 9). And from this Divine viewpoint Ahab was weighed in the balances and found seriously wanting. His introduction of the Baal cult into Israel as the state religion represents the most deliberate and devastating defection from Jehovah that history had known. As Dean Farrar observed, when we learn what Baal was and how he was worshipped, we are not surprised at the stern condemnation of Scripture. 'Half Sun-god, half Bacchus, half Hercules, Baal was worshipped under the image of a bull, the symbol of the male power of generation. In the wantonness of his rites he was akin to Peor, in their cruel atrocity to the kindred Moloch; in the demand for victims to be sacrificed to the horrible consecration of lust and blood he resembled the Minotaur, the wallowing "infamy of Crete," with its yearly tribute of youths and maidens.' This was the bestial orgy that Ahab and his murderous queen Jezebel preferred to the pure praise of Jehovah. No wonder the Lord's anger was kindled and waxed hot.

The tragedy was that the people apparently loved to have it so. Only a minority refrained from the adoration of Baal. The ancient faith of Israel was now proscribed. The prophets of the Lord were hunted out and done to death. We learn at the outset of this Eighteenth Chapter how one hundred of them were only spared through the intervention of Obadiah the governor, who hid them in a cave and sustained them with bread and water. The first great persecution had set in.

It was in the face of such a dispiriting state of affairs as this that Elijah began his ministry. Times could hardly have been worse. Yet it was through this rugged man of the hills, whose faith was invincible because the Lord was with him, that revival was to visit the land. His whole personality somehow flamed with Pentecostal incandescence. 'And Elias the prophet stood up as fire' says Ecclesiasticus, 'and his word was burning as a torch.' God matched the messenger to the moment. An Elijah is demanded by a Jezebel. 'The loftiest and sternest spirit of the true faith is raised up,' wrote Dean Stanley, in his *Lectures on the Jewish Church*, 'face to face with the proudest and fiercest spirit of the old Asiatic paganism.'

So far the verge of revival appears unauspicious in the extreme. No glimmer of hope hovers on the horizon.

That is often the case. Revival has more often followed the black days of faith than the bright. The Lord is able to save by many or by few. Meanwhile, God was shaping the instrument of His will. Elijah had evidently been poring over the Word of God and was arrested by a passage from Deuteronomy 11. 13-17. It is so significant in this context that it bears citation in full. 'And it shall come to pass, if ye shall hearken diligently unto My commandments which I command you this day, to love the Lord your God, and to serve Him with all your heart and with all your soul, that I will give you the rain of your land in his due season, the first rain and the latter rain, that thou mayest gather in thy corn, and thy wine, and thine oil. And I will send grass in thy fields for thy cattle, that thou mayest eat and be full. Take heed to yourselves, that your heart be not deceived, and ye turn aside, and serve other gods, and worship them; and then the Lord's wrath be kindled against you, and He shut up the heaven, that there be no rain, and that the land yield not her fruit; and lest ye perish quickly from off the good land which the Lord giveth you.' It was with this Scripture in mind that Elijah 'prayed earnestly that it might not rain' (James 5. 17). It was a terrible request: but then the condition of Israel was equally disturbing. So, boldly and nothing wavering, Elijah asked that God's Word might be fulfilled. When he had no doubt prayed through to the assurance that what the Lord had said would actually come to pass, he made a public announcement of the impending drought. And then, obeying the Divine command, he retired from the scene. For three and a half years there was no messenger of Jehovah in the whole of Israel. There was 'a famine in the land, not a famine of bread, nor a thirst for water, but of hearing the words of the Lord' (Amos 8. 11). At length, still under the mandate of the Almighty, Elijah emerged from his seclusion and summoned a national assembly on Carmel. He appealed to the multitude to settle the issue there and then. 'How long halt ye between two opinions? if the Lord be God, follow Him: but if Baal, then follow him' (v. 21). But there was no response. It was the awful silence of guilt. And so the trial of strength ensued between the four hundred and fifty prophets of Baal and the single-handed but God-empowered servant of the Lord. Notice the nature of the test. It is highly significant in relation to revival. 'The God that answereth by fire, let Him be God' (v. 24). The Author of Pentecostal flame was to be hailed as supreme.

The unique position of Elijah in the prophetic scheme and the fact that he is associated with the last days before the Lord's return (cf. Malachi 4. 5) combine to underline his incalculable importance in the matter of revival. No figure in the Old Testament dispensation is more instructive in this respect. Here in this passage we can discern four features which characterise the people of God on the verge of revival. When these factors were to the fore, '*then* the fire fell.' This is the climate of revival, as it were. This is the atmosphere which favours the Pentecostal kindling. That is not to say that a spiritual awakening will inevitably or automatically follow upon the appearance of these attitudes. We must still wait on God to send the fire. The time, the deed and the manner are alike His. But it is in such a spirit as these verses portray that God's people are to plead for the blessing, and the testimony of the Word and of previous history unite to inform us that this is the invariable prelude to revival.

On the verge of revival SACRIFICE IS UNRESERVED. The self-offering of believers is without restriction. All is laid on the altar. What is described in these verses from 1 Kings 18. 36-39 'came to pass at the time of the offering of the evening sacrifice.' Elijah scheduled his dramatic appeal to coincide with the hour of oblation. His action was in strict accord with the order of worship appointed in the Law, and the people were thus reminded of what they had abandoned in favour of their idolatries.

Sacrifice is an indispensable element in revival. There is an offering to be made. Revival is never undemanding. It is a costly boon and unless believers are prepared to present themselves upon the altar they had better not pray for it. God might very well answer our request and send leanness to our souls. The Scriptures tell us what is the sacrifice that God requires and approves. 'The sacrifices of God are a broken spirit: a broken and a contrite heart, O God, Thou wilt not despise' (Psalm 51. 17). But notice that the Psalmist is immediately able to pray, 'Do good in Thy good pleasure unto Zion; build Thou the walls of Jerusalem' (v. 18). God can only bless us and build us up when the sacrifice of unreserved contrition and surrender has been duly offered. There resides the secret of power.

When Mrs. Booth-Clibborn—the Maréchale—first went to France she was given a special anointing for the task of evangelising the Christless multitudes. She herself discloses the source of such unusual unction. 'When I went to France I said to Jesus, "I will suffer anything if You will give me the keys." And if I am asked what was the secret of our power in France, I answer: "First, love; second, love; third, love." And if you ask how to get it, I answer: "First, by sacrifice; second, by sacrifice; third, by sacrifice".' That is the only way. 'Nothing less than "a living sacrifice" is demanded'; declares Joseph Pearce, 'not a loan but a gift; not a compromise but a sacrifice; not our poorest but our best; not a dead but a living offering. Each drop of our blood, each ounce of our energy, each throb of our heart we must offer to God.'

On the verge of revival ENTREATY IS FERVENT. Supplications are made without ceasing to God as believers plead for the promise of revival. We cannot return too often to this emphasis on prayer. It may seem to some that writers on revival are continually harping on this one theme, but it is at once so vital and so sadly neglected that it must be kept unremittingly in view. These words of Elijah are in fact a prayer. Before the fire fell this godly man besought the Giver of every good and perfect gift to bestow the blessing. He entreated God to answer by fire. And if we are tempted to suppose that the prophet was endowed with special gifts which we do not and cannot possess, we shall do well to turn again to James 5. 16, 17. 'The effectual fervent prayer of a righteous man availeth much. Elias was a man subject to like passions as we are.' His prayer proceeded from a nature like our own.

Revival is not to be looked for unless God's people are filled with the spirit of grace and supplication. We must cry with Isaiah: 'For Zion's sake will I not hold my peace, and for Jerusalem's sake I will not rest, until the righteousness thereof go forth as brightness, and the salvation thereof as a lamp that burneth' (Isaiah 62. 1). Such prayer perseveres. It will not be put off. It presses through to victory. In the words of William Arthur, 'Prayer which takes the fact that the past prayers have not yet been answered as a reason for langour, has already ceased to be the prayer of faith. To the latter the fact that prayers remain unanswered is only evidence that the moment of the answer is so much nearer. From first to last, the lessons and examples of our Lord all tell us that prayer which cannot persevere, and urge its plea importunately, and renew, and renew itself again, and gather strength from every past petition, is not the prayer that will prevail.'

It is by patient persistence that prayer waxes fervent.

Heat cannot be generated in a moment. It is a consequence of prior activity. As one of the old Scots writers has said, the chariot wheel grows warm by rolling. We need a whole army of entreating Elijahs to maintain the fervour of prayer if revival is to come. Revival is not something that is worked up: it is something that is prayed down. 'When God intends great mercy for His people,' declared Matthew Henry, 'the first thing He does is to set them a-praying.'

On the verge of revival OBEDIENCE IS IMPLICIT. God's commands are fulfilled unhesitatingly. What He decrees is done. His Word is accepted as absolute. Nothing He lays upon His children is left unheeded. Elijah asked that it might be made known that he was God's servant and that he had 'done all these things at Thy Word.' Elijah was the slave of Jehovah. Obedience was the keynote of his character. His signature tune, as it were, by which he identified himself before his hearers, is contained in the formula, 'As the Lord God of Israel liveth, before whom I stand . . .' (1 Kings 17. 1; 18. 15).

Alexander Maclaren had a remarkable sermon on Elijah standing before the Lord. In it he showed how those words reflect the utter obedience of the prophet to the Divine behest. 'He professes that he stands before the Lord, girt for His service, watching to be guided by His eye, and ready to run when He bids.' Such unswerving obedience is essential to revival. Indeed, it is the very core of revival. Those who deprecate what they superciliously describe as 'revivalism' usually assume that excitement and disorder are its chief concomitants. They confuse the accidents with the essence. As Ernest Baker has wisely remarked, 'A revival may produce noise, but it does not consist of it. The real thing is whole-hearted obedience.'

One of the most convincing demonstrations of revival

in our time has occurred in East Africa, in the Ruanda
territory. Dr. Joe Church, a medical missionary, has
told how it all began. He came down to the coast some
years ago frustrated and hungry for God. Here he met an
African Christian who was praying that the promise of
Joel 2. 28 concerning the final outpouring of the Spirit
might be fulfilled. Together he and Dr. Church thumbed
the pages of a Scofield Bible and tracked down every
reference to the Holy Ghost. They reached Acts 5. 32—
'So is also the Holy Ghost, Whom God hath given to them
that obey Him.' 'This was riveted in my mind,' said Dr.
Church. 'Nobody came to me with five points on revival
or with a formula. And I have found that when people try
to copy revival or anything spiritual, they get off the
centre. Revival cannot be copied. It must be repeated.
Christ is the centre. Christ is revival when He has full
sway in the human heart.' Obedience is the key.

On the verge of revival SELF IS EXCLUDED. Men are
nothing: Christ is all. Human personalities recede from
view that God may dominate the scene. The prophet's
approach to God in this moving prayer was marked by
self-effacement. Elijah was ready to take a back seat, as
we say. 'Hear me, O Lord, hear me,' he pleaded, with a
passionate intensity of desire, 'that this people may know
that Thou art the Lord God.' Self is forgotten in this
mighty and prevailing prayer. As Matthew Henry
observes, Elijah is concerned with two things only—the
glory of God and the edification of the people.

Such a selfless spirit is necessary to revival. Only when
God's glory is all our aim shall we see a gracious renewal
in our midst. Only when the salvation of sinners and the
recovery of backsliders is our continued burden shall we
behold the Pentecostal day again. In such a passionate
concern all consideration of self will be swallowed up.
'Let my name be blighted', cried Danton, the French

patriot, 'let France be free!' That is how the earnest believer will feel about the lost sheep of God's house. The heart of Moses bled for the children of Israel when they lapsed into idolatry. 'Oh this people have sinned a great sin, and have made them gods of gold. Yet now, if Thou wilt forgive their sin—and if not, blot me, I pray Thee, out of Thy book which Thou hast written' (Exodus 32. 31, 32). Paul shared the same longing: 'For I could wish that myself were accursed from Christ for my brethren, my kinsmen according to the flesh' (Romans 9. 3). Self must be buried if believers are to have power with God.

This 37th verse also reveals the innermost nature of revival. 'That this people may know that Thou art the Lord God, and that Thou hast turned their heart back again.' That is revival. It is God turning back the hearts of His wandering children. It is God leading His faithless ones to repentance. It is God drawing His own to Himself once more, 'with cords of a man, with bands of love' (Hosea 11. 4).

Such, then, is the verge of revival. It was instantly followed by blessing. 'Then the fire of the Lord fell, and consumed the burnt sacrifice.' God visited Carmel in wonder-working power. And what was the consequence? It was the acknowledgement of God. 'And when all the people saw it, they fell on their faces: and they said, The Lord, He is the God; the Lord, He is the God.' That is always the result of revival. It brings a new recognition of the Divine sovereignty. Its purpose is fulfilled as believers and unbelievers together are constrained to cry: 'To God be the glory! great things He hath done!' And it leads to even fuller blessing. The God Who had answered by fire soon answered also by rain and by the overthrow of Ahab's iniquitous regime. What Elijah began, Jehu completed and 'destroyed Baal out of

Israel' (2 Kings 10. 28). So at length it could be said,
'Know now that there shall fall unto the earth nothing of
the word of the Lord, which the Lord spake concerning
the house of Ahab: for the Lord hath done that which
He spake by His servant Elijah' (2 Kings 10. 10).

CHAPTER VII

THE HOUR OF REVIVAL

'Now when Solomon had made an end of praying, the fire came down from heaven, and consumed the burnt offering and the sacrifices; and the glory of the Lord filled the house.'

—2 Chronicles 7. 1

THE name of Evan Roberts is for ever linked with revival. He was the Divinely chosen leader of the great Welsh awakening at the beginning of this present century. It was through this Spirit-filled, sanctified man that blessing was brought to thousands. However, we shall focus our gaze now not on Evan Roberts himself but on Evan Roberts's Bible. It became almost as famous as he was. A picture of it went around the world. It was no ordinary copy of the Scriptures. As you examined it you could see that it had been scorched by flames. It had obviously survived a fire of some sort. When Evan Roberts was a young man he had been a miner. He was once involved in a colliery explosion. His body was spared injury, but his Bible, which lay beside him, was burnt and charred. And the page where it stood open on that day of disaster was precisely that which confronts us now. Evan Roberts often used to search the Scriptures down the pit and on this momentous occasion he had been meditating upon Solomon's mighty supplication and its even mightier consequences in the quickening of God's people. These chapters in Second Chronicles were to play a prominent part in the Welsh revival, as they have done at other seasons of refreshing from the Lord's hand. If we are eager to learn still more from the Word concerning the manner of such visitation, this verse can teach us much, for it speaks of the hour of revival. It deals with the actual advent of blessing.

It follows the solemn dedication of Solomon's temple. At a holy convocation of all the children of Israel the sacred ark was carried into the newly completed sanctuary together with the tabernacle of the congregation and all the consecrated vessels. After joyful praise had been offered to the Lord, the king blessed the people and glorified God. Then he uttered his great prayer of thankfulness and intercession—one of the peak passages of all Scripture (2 Chronicles 6. 12-42). The verse which holds our attention now opens the Seventh Chapter of Second Chronicles, immediately after Solomon has concluded his moving peroration. 'Now, my God, let, I beseech Thee, Thine eyes be open, and let Thine ears be attent unto the prayer that is made in this place. Now therefore arise, O Lord God, into Thy resting place, Thou, and the ark of Thy strength: let Thy priests, O Lord God, be clothed with salvation, and let Thy saints rejoice in goodness. O Lord God, turn not away the face of Thine anointed: remember the mercies of David Thy servant' (2 Chronicles 6. 40-42). The section which describes the sending of fire from heaven is peculiar to the Book of Chronicles. It does not appear in the parallel version in 1 Kings 8. As we have already realised, the Holy Spirit has spoken through the pages of Chronicles in an unusually revealing way concerning the nature of revival. This paragraph in 2 Chronicles 7. 1-3 is a case in point, filling up as it does the gap between verses 61 and 62 of 1 Kings 8.

Let us then look more closely at this important text as it speaks about the hour of revival. No doubt at school you were sometimes given a simple test during the English lesson. A passage of prose was set before you—culled from some classical author—and in order to discover whether the pupils could pick out its essential meaning, you would be required to underline what you considered to be the key words. We shall do that now with this verse, with the aid of the Interpreter Spirit. We shall take up an imaginary pen and mark the places where the stresses of this sentence fall. See how it reads: 'Now when Solomon had made an end of *praying*, the *fire* came down from heaven, and *consumed* the burnt offering and the sacrifices; and the *glory* of the Lord filled the house.' We will extract those four vital words and concentrate upon them, for they contain the secret of revival—Praying, Fire, Consumed, Glory.

PRAYING: THAT WORD SPEAKS OF THE PREFACE TO REVIVAL. 'Now when Solomon had made an end of *praying*.' There can be no awakening without fervent prayer. To expect God to bless where we do not pray is to ask Him to act contrary to His Word. Throughout the Scriptures He expressly invites us to call upon Him. 'Seek the Lord and His strength, seek His face continually' (1 Chronicles 16. 11). 'Seek ye the Lord while He may be found, call ye upon Him while He is near' (Isaiah 55. 6). 'Call upon Me in the day of trouble: I will deliver thee, and thou shalt glorify Me' (Psalm 50. 15). We are to ask that we may receive, seek that we may find, and knock that the door may be opened. We are to make our requests known unto God and to pray without ceasing. And our heavenly Father firmly promises to respond to the cry of His children. 'And it shall come to pass, that before they call, I will answer; and while they are yet speaking, I will hear' (Isaiah 65. 24). But if God's people fail to pray we can hardly hope for help.

The history of revivals proves the truth of this simple law of spiritual cause and effect. God's quickening has been bestowed in response to earnest, heartfelt and unremitting prayer. Every great religious awakening can be traced to at least one kneeling figure. But such prayer must be pure and passionate. It must be persistent and importunate. It must cry, 'I will not let Thee go, except Thou bless me' (Genesis 32. 36). The trouble so often is that our prayers are not nearly urgent enough. We have not yet resisted unto blood nor have we agonised unto sweat. Only Gethsemane pleadings will prevail. 'Beware of prayerless tears', someone has said, 'and tearless prayers.' We need to share the Master's spirit, 'Who in the days of His flesh, when He had offered up prayers and supplications with strong crying and tears unto Him that was able to save Him from death, and was heard in that He feared; though He were a Son, yet learned He obedience by the things which He suffered' (Hebrews 5. 6, 7). Are we so concerned for the salvation of sinners that we can plead with Jeremiah: 'But if ye will not hear it, my soul shall weep in secret places for your pride; and mine eye shall weep sore, and run down with tears, because the Lord's flock is carried away captive' (Jeremiah 13. 17)?

Consider just two instances of this crucial relationship between prayer and revival. The name of David Brainerd does not even rank in the listings of *Encyclopaedia Britannica* yet that intrepid missionary to the Red Indians was one of the greatest revival pioneers of all time. By his consecrated endeavours an incredible transformation was effected amongst the community of American Indians in New England. The entry in Brainerd's diary for August 8th., 1745, is historic. 'In the afternoon I preached to the Indians. There was much visible concern among them. . . . God seemed to descend upon the assembly "like a rushing mighty wind," and with an astonishing energy bore down all before it. I stood amazed at the influence which seized the audience almost universally and could only compare it to a mighty torrent, or a swelling deluge, that with its insupportable weight and pressure bears down and sweeps before it whatever comes in its way.' And what was the secret behind this remarkable recurrence of Pentecostal power? Again and again Brainerd's journal bears testimony to his unflagging constancy in prayer. He had been wrestling for the blessing over many months. 'His whole life was one of burning prayer to God for the American Indians,' writes E. M. Bounds. 'By day and by night he prayed. Before preaching and after preaching he prayed. On his bed of straw he prayed. Retiring to the dense and lonely forests he fasted and prayed. Hour by hour, day after day, early morn and late at night, he was praying and fasting, pouring out his soul, interceding, communing with God. He was with God mightily in prayer, and God was with him mightily, and by it he being dead yet speaketh and worketh and will speak and work till the end comes and among the glorious ones of that glorious day he will be with the first.'

The other illustration of this kinship between prayer and revival is within the present century. An exceptionally fruitful movement of the Spirit took place at a station of the China Inland Mission and attracted no little attention. Both in numbers and in quality the converts were unusual. No other area under the supervision of the society could match it. Where lay the explanation? Dr. Hudson Taylor, the renowned founder of the Mission, was completely mystified until eventually the secret came to light when he visited a certain English town for a meeting. At the close, a man approached Hudson Taylor and introduced himself. Taylor was amazed at his accurate and detailed knowledge of this particular station where such a wonderful work of grace was going forward. 'How is it,' he asked, 'that you know so intimately this Mission Station and its people?' 'Why,' the man replied, 'the missionary is an old college chum of mine. For years we have been corresponding. He sends me the names of the enquirers and converts and these I have daily taken to God in prayer.' Dr. Taylor added: 'This was the secret of revival.' A praying saint at home, specifically interceding for the needs of that distant place, accounted for the outbreak of blessing. Mary Slessor once explained the effectiveness of her own ministry by saying that 'prayer-waves pulsate all the way from Great Britain to Calabar.'

> 'Away in foreign lands they wondered how
> Their simple word had power:
> At home the Christians, two or three, had met
> To pray an hour.'

Prayer is the preface to revival. 'Now when Solomon had made an end of praying, the fire came down from heaven.' The Holy Spirit convicts the Church of negligence in this indispensable obligation. 'When I get to heaven,' said Moody, 'next to the wonder of seeing my Saviour will be, I think, the wonder that I made so little use of the power of prayer.'

The second emphasis of this verse is on FIRE: THAT WORD SPEAKS OF THE ESSENCE OF REVIVAL. 'The *fire* came down from heaven.' Revival is a fiery phenomenon. Our God is the God Who answers by fire. There are other evidences of that fact besides Carmel. When Moses and Aaron 'went into the tabernacle of the congregation, and came out, and blessed the people,' we read that 'there came a *fire* out from before the Lord' (Leviticus 9. 23, 24). When Gideon laid his offering of flesh and unleavened cakes upon the rock, 'then the angel of the Lord put forth the end of the staff that was in his hand, and touched the flesh and the unleavened cakes; and there rose up *fire* out of the rock' (Judges 6. 21). When David built an altar on the threshing floor of Ornan, 'and offered burnt offerings and peace offerings, and called upon the Lord, He answered him from heaven by *fire*' (1 Chronicles 21. 26). 'I am come to send *fire* on the earth,' declared the Lord Jesus Christ, 'and what will I if it be already kindled?' (Luke 12. 49). And on the day of Pentecost, when the Spirit was poured out upon the company, 'there appeared unto them cloven tongues like as of *fire*, and it sat upon each of them' (Acts 2. 3).

Revival is well described as fire. It is the work of God Himself, and He is a flaming fire. He blazed at Sinai and in the burning bush. Fire *cleanses*. It refines and purifies. The metal is only separated from the ore by a fierce heat. Revival is a cleansing process. It burns up the dross of base desire and makes the mountains flow. It gives the Church and the world a moral spring-clean. Fire *warms*. It glows. It transmits heat to all around. Revival brings new fervour to the cold and indifferent. It renews the warmth of fellowship within the Church and gives believers a fresh ardour in testifying to those that are without. Fire *lights*. It affords illumination. It sheds a cheerful beam in a shadowy place. Revival leads us deeper into spiritual truth. It shows us more of God. It confirms the things that remain and causes fresh light and truth to break forth from His holy Word. Fire *spreads*. It is contagious. It gets out of hand. It cannot be controlled by human intervention. Revival enjoys a like liberty. It runs its own course. No man-made restrictions can confine it. One loving heart sets another on fire. When it gets under way nothing can stop it.

Fire is one of the original elements. It cannot be manufactured. It is the gift of God. Revival is like that. It cannot be prefabricated. It is a Divine creation. It does not emerge or arise out of the human environment. It cannot be conjured up. It is sent from above. Like the fire in Scripture, it falls.

'See how great a flame aspires,
Kindled by a spark of grace!
Jesu's love the nations fires,
Sets the kingdoms on a blaze.
To bring fire on earth He came;
Kindled in some hearts it is;
O that all might catch the flame,
All partake the glorious bliss!'

'The fire came down from heaven': that is the Scripture account of revival. How exact it is!

The next stress of this verse falls on the verb CONSUMED: THAT WORD SPEAKS OF THE COST OF REVIVAL. 'And *consumed* the burnt offering and the sacrifices.' Our God is a consuming fire. When the fire of revival falls it eats up all our burnt offerings and sacrifices. All must be laid on the altar in such an hour and all will be utterly devoured by the leaping flames. In each of the instances we noted earlier where God answered by fire this word 'consumed' occurs or is implied. Elijah: 'Then the fire of the Lord fell, and *consumed* the burnt sacrifice, and the wood, and the stones, and the dust, and licked up the water that was in the trench' (1 Kings 18. 38). Moses and Aaron: 'And there came a fire out from before the Lord, and *consumed* upon the altar the burnt offering and the fat' (Leviticus 9. 24). Gideon: 'And there rose up fire out of the rock, and *consumed* the flesh and the unleavened cakes' (Judges 6. 21). David: 'He answered him from heaven by fire *upon the altar of burnt offering*' (1 Chronicles 21. 26). The fire always falls on the altar where our offering is laid and completely consumes it.

In a season of revival nothing can be kept back by God's elect. It is no time for half-hearted or even three-quarter hearted disciples. We must be what Frances Ridley Havergal used to call 'all for Jesus Christians.' He who gave all for us demands all from us. Even the dearest idol we have known has to be thrown into the relentless

flames. There must be an Ephesian bonfire in our hearts.
Perhaps for those within the institutional churches the
hardest thing we have to sacrifice is our reputation.
Let us face it. If we go right into the adventure of revival
for God, we shall offend our friends. Even our nominally
Christian companions will draw in their skirts. We shall
lose caste with them. We shall be regarded as speckled
birds. If we are to obey God in this matter rather than
men we may forfeit the good opinion of those within the
Church who have not yet caught a vision of revival as
God's answer to the world's need.

There came a period in the life of Charles Haddon
Spurgeon when he was subjected to attacks and accus-
ations of every sort because of his fidelity to the fulness of
the Gospel and his yearning to take it to the people
where they were. Very occasionally he alluded to this
fiery trial from the pulpit. In a sermon in 1857 he said:
'I shall never forget the circumstance when, after I
thought I had made a full consecration to Christ, a
slanderous report against my character came to my ears,
and my heart was broken in agony because I should have
to lose that, in preaching Christ's Gospel. I fell on my
knees, and said, '"Master, I will not keep back even my
character from Thee. If I must lose that too, then let it
go; it is the dearest thing I have; but it shall go, if, like
my Master, they shall say that I have a devil, and am
mad".'

There is no escape. The whole burnt offering and the
entire sacrifice of ourselves must be laid upon the altar to
be consumed by the fire from heaven. John Calvin's
motto must be ours. His crest was a burning heart, with
the words, 'I give Thee all: I keep back nothing for
myself.'

The final key word of this verse is GLORY: THAT WORD
SPEAKS OF THE OBJECT OF REVIVAL. 'And the *glory* of the

Lord filled the house.' The impact of such a manifestation is indicated by what followed. 'And the priests could not enter the house of the Lord, because the glory of the Lord had filled the Lord's house. And when all the children of Israel saw how the fire came down, and the glory of the Lord upon the house, they bowed themselves with their faces to the ground upon the pavement, and worshipped and praised the Lord, saying, For He is good; for His mercy endureth for ever' (2 Chronicles 7. 2, 3). The final aim of revival is not to exalt man. The final aim is revival is not even to redeem man. The final aim of revival is that God may be glorified. It remains true, of course, that He is supremely magnified in the salvation of sinners, but the rescue of the lost is not an end in itself. It is a means to His glory, that God may be all in all.

The Scripture consistently associates the glory of God with the symbol of fire. At Sinai 'the sight of the glory of the Lord was like devouring fire on the top of the mount in the eyes of the children of Israel' (Exodus 24. 17). And in each of the examples already quoted where God answers by fire and consumes the sacrifice, His glory is revealed. Let us go through them yet again, for they are richly instructive. Elijah: 'And when all the people saw it, they *fell on their faces*: and they said, The Lord, He is the God; the Lord, He is the God' (1 Kings 18. 39). Moses and Aaron: 'and the *glory* of the Lord appeared unto all the people . . . which when all the people saw, they shouted, and *fell on their faces*' (Leviticus 9. 23, 24. Gideon: 'Alas! O Lord God, for because I have seen an *angel* of the Lord face to face' (Judges 6. 22). David: 'And the Lord commanded the *angel*; and he put up his sword again into the sheath thereof' (1 Chronicles 21. 27). The sequence is the same throughout—fire, sacrifice, glory.

The great object of revival is the glory of Almighty

God. There must be no other end in view amongst those who seek the outpouring of the Spirit. Believers must purge themselves of every baser motive. *Soli Deo gloria*—to the only glory of God—must be our slogan, as it was of the Protestant Reformers. Every preparation for the coming Pentecost has to be directed towards this single objective. 'Prepare ye the way of the Lord, make straight in the desert a highway for our God. . . . And the glory of the Lord shall be revealed' (Isaiah 40. 4, 5). Nine years after the Cambuslang revival of 1742, the minister, William McCulloch, wrote a long letter describing that memorable work of the Spirit. This is how he concludes. 'When I mention such comfortable abiding effects of this work, I would not have it ascribed to any creature, but that the entire glory of it should be given to God whose work it was. It is true, there were many ministers here, from places near and more remote; and some of them of great eminence, who preached here at my desire, and who also joined with me in exhortation to souls appearing in spiritual distress, who resorted to the manse. But what could all these avail without the Divine power and blessing? Whoever plant and water, it is God that gives the increase. Ministers are but instruments in His hands. . . . It is very fit and reasonable that he that builds the temple should bear the glory: and Christ is both the foundation and founder of the Church, and therefore let all the glory be ascribed to Him.' Glory is always the grand objective of revival. So our prayer must be:

> 'Revive Thy work, O Lord,
>   And give refreshing showers;
> The glory shall be all Thine own,
>   The blessing, Lord, be ours.'

CHAPTER VIII

THE MARKS OF REVIVAL

'And they went forth, and preached every where, the Lord working with them, and confirming the word with signs following.' —Mark 16. 20

THE last two verses of the Gospel according to Mark present a striking contrast. We read first of our Lord's glorious Ascension to the right hand of God and then of the witness of the apostles here on earth. It would seem that there is a great gulf fixed between these spheres of operation. But the Evangelist would clearly have us understand that there is an intimate relationship between them. There is a very real connection between the exalted Saviour and the labouring missionaries of the Cross. They are in fact continuing the task He Himself began to undertake in the days of His flesh. And, what is more, it is under His direction and with His co-operation that the work of the infant Church proceeds. It is the same Lord Who was 'received up into heaven' (v. 19) Who is found to be 'working with them' (v. 20). It is He, moreover, Who confirms the word with signs following. He sets His own seal to their endeavours by distinguishing them from any merely human achievements. 'And so the Gospel which pre-eminently sets forth the power and activity of the Son of God on earth,' comments Graham Swift, 'closes with the revelation of the unfinished task of the Church on earth. That task still awaits completion, but the same Lord still works with those who obey His command, confirming the word with signs following.'

This is an obvious reference to the Pentecost revival. One of its recorded results was that 'many wonders and

signs were done by the apostles' (Acts 2. 43). Again:
'And with great power gave the apostles witness of the
resurrection of the Lord Jesus: and great grace was upon
them all' (Acts 4. 33). And yet again: 'And by the hands
of the apostles were many signs and wonders wrought
amongst the people' (Acts 5. 12). The word translated
'sign' is a most interesting one. It is a favourite term of
John in his Gospel and it suggests something more than
simply a miracle. There is an arrow running through it
indicating the source of such a demonstration of Divine
power. 'It is involved and declared in the very word.'
said Archbishop Trench, in his *Synonyms of the New
Testament*, 'that the prime object and end of the miracle
is to lead us to something out of and beyond itself; that,
so to speak, it is a kind of finger-post of God, pointing for
us to this (Isaiah 7. 11; 38. 7); valuable, not so much for
what it is, as for that which it indicates of the grace and
power of the doer, or of the immediate connection with a
higher spiritual world in which He stands (Mark 16. 20;
Acts 14. 3; Hebrews 2. 4; Exodus 7. 9, 10; 1 Kings 13. 3).'
It is in this extended sense that the 'signs' following to
confirm the Word must be interpreted. They represent
the distinctive marks of revival. This is how it is recognised when it comes.

There is a question which should seriously concern the
Church today. It is this—Would we know what revival
was if God chose to send it and would we want it if it
arrived? When we pray for awakening, do we really
understand what we are requesting? It may be that the
Lord Jesus Christ is meeting our uninformed pleadings
for revival with the reply He gave to the mother of James
and John in Mark 20. 22—'Ye know not what ye ask.'
Maybe before the blessing can descend we shall have to
be emancipated from our preconceived notions of what it
ought to be like.

In his challenging little booklet on *Continuous Revival*, Norman P. Grubb acknowledged that his contact with the Ruanda awakening in East Africa revolutionised his ideas on the subject. He told how he first heard two of the Ruanda Christians speaking very quietly and simply in London to some ninety members on the staff of a missionary society. At the final session they opened the door for anyone present to say anything that was on their hearts. Very soon one and another were bringing into the light areas in their own lives where they had come face to face with sin which had before been unobserved and which now they placed beneath the cleansing blood of Christ. Norman Grubb said that he got a sudden shock at the close when one of the two remarked, 'I don't know if you realize it, friends, but this *is* revival!'

Are we certain we would recognise revival if we saw it? John Wesley once preached a celebrated sermon on 'The Marks of the New Birth.' It might be well for us to notice the marks of revival, for, after all, revival is to the whole body of Christians what regeneration is to the individual.

Let us begin with the negative. Let us note what revival is not. There is a glorious freedom about God's sovereign work in spiritual quickening. It is due to the operation of the Holy Spirit, 'and where the Spirit of the Lord is, there is liberty' (2 Corinthians 3. 17). This manifests itself in an unmistakable independence of man and the man-made. Revival is all of God and plainly advertises itself as such. It is *independent of organisation*. It is not a stunt. It is not a publicity project. It is not even a well-planned evangelistic crusade. We thank God for all the wise preparation that is put into such ventures and we firmly believe that evangelism is the continuous task of the Church. But no amount of organisation can produce a revival. Techniques are helpless here. The only plan that counts in revival is God's and He does not disclose it in advance. A genuine movement of the Spirit is seen to be such because of its incommensurability with any purely human contrivance. It is essentially disparate. It stands self-authenticated as Divine. It springs from no earth-born ingenuity but from the mind of the Maker Himself. 'If you would appreciate the sublime relations of revivals of religion,' wrote Dr. E. N. Kirk in his lectures on the subject, 'accustom yourselves to trace the movement of those high and dreadful wheels of Ezekiel's vision. They are instinct with the Spirit of God. Their wings are high and awful; they are full of eyes; the purposes of Divine wisdom, and the energy of the Divine will, directing the events which prepare the way of the Lord when He comes in revival.' And when the fire falls, it is known to be of God and not of men. It distinguishes itself immediately and incontrovertibly from its counterfeit. Samuel Chadwick warned his generation against what he called 'stage fire.' We still need to be on our guard against an artificial conflagration which may deserve the name of revivalism but never of revival.

Again, revival is *independent of personalities*. It is not focussed upon any one individual or group of individuals. It does not rely on the magic of a famous name. Man is often the instrument, but God is the sovereign originator of all renewal. The only Person who matters is the Holy Ghost. God the Father has committed the miracle of revival to the Spirit so that the Son may perform His saving office and be exalted. But quickening itself is the prerogative of the Comforter and thus His is the supreme Personality in this regard. Every true revival reflects this trait. So powerful was the impact of the Holy Spirit at Philippi that Paul and Silas could take their departure after only a two-day mission, confident that the work would continue (Acts 16. 13-40). Discussing the determinative factor in revival, Calvin Colton came to this conclusion. 'It is not the eloquence of man. It is God that speaketh—it is God that is heard—it is God that is felt. A George Whitefield might pass along, and draw the world around him, and make a deep impression; and sinners, here and there, might be converted through his instrumentality. But the moment he is gone, the religious atmosphere goes with him. Not so in a genuine revival of religion. It came not of man, and it is dependent on no accident of this sort. Instruments, to be sure, may help or hinder it, may beautify or mar it, may render it as the garden of God, or disfigure it, and sow tares, and plant much evil fruit. These accidents may and do affect the work, but they do not annihilate its peculiar character.' God says, 'I will work, and who shall let it?' (Isaiah 43. 13). Neither the frailty of His servants nor the devices of His foes can hinder Him. The verdict of Dr. R. W. Dale of Birmingham on the Moody Mission in Britain in 1875 bears repetition: 'The work was most plainly of God, for I could see no real relation between the men and what they have done.'

Moreover, revival is *independent of evangelism*. We need to distinguish between these terms. They are too often confused. Evangelism is spoken of as if it were revival and revival is spoken of as if it were evangelism. In the first case, abnormal success in soul-winning is mistaken for the Pentecostal cloudburst. In the second, revival is erroneously identified with a crusade for conversions. Not that evangelism is to be decried or its value in any way minimised. It is vital and necessary and must be maintained. But revival is something utterly different. When the Church takes the Gospel to the people, that is evangelism. When the people come to the Church for the Gospel, that is revival. Revival is more than an intensive mission. It is more than a colossal campaign.

Revival carries all before it as a flood and sweeps men into the kingdom in numbers greater than any crusade could cope with. Sometimes churches are so sold on evangelism that they see no need for revival. Then it is necessary to remove the rewards of the one that the other and greater may be sought. God deals in diverse manners with His people in order to train them for His will.

So much for the negative. Now let us proceed to the positive. We have space only to mention briefly the five great marks of revival in every age. Pray over them. Agonise about them. Shed tears for them. Plead with God that these may once again become the signs following the Word within Christ's Church.

The first mark of revival is PRAYERFULNESS. That must stand first because it is first. Prayer characterises the beginning, continuance and final consummation of revival. Revival is shot through and through with all-prevailing prayer. We cannot possibly over-emphasise the part played by prayer in spiritual awakening. Revival only comes when the Church contains its Daniels whose windows are open towards Jerusalem. And revival only remains whilst such intercession is sustained. The period from 1740 to 1750 was one of the most blessed in the entire religious history of Scotland, for revival broke out not only in Kilsyth and Cambuslang, but in many other places as well. A vast multitude of souls was added to the Church and throughout the entire season of refreshing the spirit of prayer was extensively prevalent. The praying societies were scattered all over the land and the incense of intercession rose from many a kneeling band. Meanwhile the spiritual glow that was kindled in England under the inspired ministry of the Wesleys and Whitefield was maintained in innumerable gatherings for the fellowship of prayer. During the awakening on the island of Lewis from 1824 to 1835 visitors overheard the passionate pleadings of the people at all hours of the day. 'Many a bush formed a shelter for a soul communing with its God; and along the brown ridges of the fallow, by stooping so as to cast the figures between the eye and the clear margin of the horizon, dim forms might be discerned, either alone, or two or three together, kneeling and pouring out their wants at the footstool of mercy.' So runs a contemporary report. At the time of the 1858 revival in the United States of America there was 'a prayer meeting two thousand miles long,' according to a traveller who had made his way from Omaha to Boston. Evan Roberts used to show visitors the worn rug on his study floor where sometimes for whole nights he would kneel to intercede for the soul of Wales. The Welsh revival of 1904 was much more a time of praying than of preaching. Many of the crowded meetings were almost wholly occupied with prayer. Here is the distinctive mark of revival. It is only born and maintained in the spirit of prayerfulness.

The second mark of revival is AWARENESS. One of the sure signs of the Spirit's presence is a new recognition of God. Indeed Duncan Campbell defined revival in these terms. It is, he asserted, 'a going of God among His people, and an awareness of God laying hold of the community.' Notice the sequence there. First God moves among His own and then those that are without become conscious of it. No need for much talking or even for much preaching: in revival unbelievers are made vividly aware of God because He is so evidently at work amongst His people. In *Man the Unknown* Dr. Alexis Carrel regrets that 'a sense of the Holy is on the way to disappearance among civilised people.' Only revival will restore it. Referring to the movement of the Spirit in Northampton, Massachusetts in 1734, Jonathan Edwards in his *Narrative* recorded that although business was not ordinarily neglected, 'yet religion was with all sorts the great concern. The thing in their view was the kingdom of heaven, and every one appeared pressing into it. There was scarce a person in the town left unconcerned. The vainest and loosest of all, and those who were used to speak most slightly of inward religion, were now generally in deep convictions. And the work increased daily more and more; so that from day to day, for many months together, might be seen evident instances of sinners brought "out of darkness into marvellous light".' Set beside that glimpse of the American scene this newspaper report from the *Glasgow Commonwealth* in 1859. 'The wonderful change that is perceptible on the very surface of society is now frequently the subject of remark. In the family party, in the bus or railway carriage, on board the steamer, in the street, on 'change, it is no longer "a strange thing" to hear people as Christians able to "give a reason for the hope that is in them," or . . . as earnest enquirers more or less audibly demanding—"What must we do to be saved"?' One of the most impressive of the signs following revival is this unusually heightened awareness of God.

The third mark of revival is BROKENNESS. This is the deepest cost of revival insofar as it affects the individual believer. Alongside all the countless benefits that spiritual quickening brings in its train there must be placed this inescapable element of brokenness. Here is the point where more than any other Christians need to bare themselves before God in naked honesty and ask whether they really desire revival at such a price. For God requires that His people shall be humbled at the Cross before He can fully bless and He requires that they should remain there if He is to go on blessing. 'The Lord is nigh unto them that are of a broken heart; and saveth such as be of a contrite spirit' (Psalm 34. 18). A missionary who had experienced revival in his work overseas commented on this feature of a genuine awakening. It was quite common, he said, for the question to be asked concerning one whose zeal was flagging, 'But is he a broken Christian?' That is the only kind of Christian God can really use at any time, but the fact becomes especially evident in a season of Pentecostal reinvigoration. According to Principal J. D. Drysdale, such brokenness comes about when the believer is faced with a double revelation: first, the revelation of God's holiness and then the revelation of his own unholiness. That was what happened to Job. Listen to his testimony. 'I have heard of Thee by the hearing of the ear: but now mine eye seeth Thee. Wherefore I abhor myself, and repent in dust and ashes' (Job 42. 5, 6). The 'wherefore' is highly significant. It suggests the causal connection between the vision of God and the brokenness of man. The one will always succeed the other.

The fourth mark of revival is OPENNESS. When the believer is broken at Calvary all his defences are down. He is now without covering in the sight of God and of his fellow-man. And indeed he has nothing to hide. We can compare a man to a house, as Norman Grubb was fond of doing. It has a roof and walls. Openness means that the roof comes off so that there is nothing between man and God, and the walls come down so that there is nothing between man and his neighbour. In revival such a two-way openness is always most noticeable. It is both vertical and horizontal. The Church stands 'naked and opened unto the eyes of Him with whom we have to do' (Hebrews 4. 13). There is no attempt at concealment from Him. And there is a constant readiness to receive all that He has to bestow. As the mouths of fledglings in the nest are ever open to be fed from the parent bird, so believers are hungry to be filled from the good hand of God. But in

revival openness is also evident in a new fellowship
between those who love the Lord. All distinctions are
rendered void. As at Pentecost, all that believe are
together and have all things common. The injunction
of the Word is obeyed: 'Confess your faults one to
another, and pray for one another' (James 5. 16). Openness is a sure sign of revival. Remember that the first sin
condemned in the Apostolic Church was the refusal of
Ananias and Sapphira to share their possessions and their
endeavour to hide their action from God and their
companions.

The fifth mark of revival is FAITHFULNESS. As we shall
see in a later chapter, revival issues in a new loyalty, a new
devotion, a new enthusiasm for God's House, God's
Word, God's Day, God's Kingdom. There is no need to
devise forward movements for the Church when revival
comes in like a flood. When men meet God in decisive
encounter, they realise without being urged that all must
be laid on the altar. They will gladly serve Him, not as
hired servants, but as sons. Revival makes the ideal real
within the Church of God. Once again, as at the
beginning, our Lord Jesus Christ presents it to Himself
'a glorious church, not having spot or wrinkle, or any
such thing; but that it should be holy and without
blemish' (Ephesians 5. 27).

These, then, are the signs following revival. This is
how we know it to be what it is. The differentiae of
Pentecost are unmistakable. The only question is whether
we are spiritually equipped for all that is involved. O
God, grant that 'Thy people shall be willing in the day
of Thy power, in the beauties of holiness' (Psalm 110. 3).

CHAPTER IX

THE PURPOSE OF REVIVAL

'Wilt Thou not revive us again: that Thy people may
rejoice in Thee? Shew us Thy mercy, O Lord, and grant us
Thy salvation.' —Psalm 85. 6, 7

A WELL-KNOWN English public school was once to
receive a distinguished visitor from the Commonwealth. A member of the staff was deputed to conduct
him round the premises. He had taken the precaution
of preparing himself with the utmost thoroughness. He
reminded himself of the long and honoured history of the
school. He was satisfied that he was fully conversant with
every statue and stained glass window and mural
inscription. When the important guest arrived the teacher
felt sure that he could answer any question that might be
put. And yet the very first enquiry floored him. It was
not at all what he had expected. Including the entire
building in one broad sweep of the hand, the visitor
asked, 'Now, tell me, what is this school for?'

In the midst of prayers and preparations for revival
and even more when the fire has actually fallen, it is vital
that Christians should know what it is for. Unless we are
aware of the purpose for which it is intended we shall
miss the mark and lose the benefit of what God bestows.
This familiar petition from the Eighty-Fifth Psalm
reminds us what God aims to do through revival. It
merits our reverent attention. It has been described by
an old commentator as a patriot's prayer. That gives it
a special relevance for the present day. This is how his
introduction runs: 'The prayer of a patriot for his
afflicted country, in which he pleads God's former

mercies, and by faith foresees better days.' The prophets and psalmists of Israel were in fact the greatest patriots of their time. Their concern for their country was expressed in earnest yearning and passionate intercession for the peace and prosperity of the homeland God Himself had given them. They knew that spiritual revival was the secret of national wellbeing and so they pleaded with the Almighty to send His showers of blessing. That is what the Psalmist is doing here. First, he praises God for all that is past. He recalls bygone days of renewal (vv. 1-3) and acknowledges the many favours shown by Jehovah in former ages. Then he begs the Lord to repeat His gracious condescension and once again to visit His people in power and love. 'Turn us O God of our salvation and cause Thine anger toward us to cease. Wilt Thou be angry with us for ever? wilt Thou draw out Thine anger to all generations?' (vv. 4 5). Then follows the heartfelt plea 'Wilt Thou not revive us again?' and immediately associated with this burning question we find an important statement about the purpose of revival. Here it is: 'that Thy people may rejoice in Thee.' That is what Pentecost is for.

The purpose of revival is THE REVEALING OF GOD'S GRACE. Its primary aim is to exalt His excellent greatness. It is intended to magnify His majesty. The 'Thou' in this verse is emphatic, as in the preceding section. It is only God who can revive and it is in Him that His people are blessed. And so the Psalmist continues: 'Shew us *Thy* mercy O Lord and grant us *Thy* salvation.' The overall objective of revival is 'that glory may dwell in our land' (v. 9).

When Pentecost occurs again there is always a fresh recognition of God's grace and greatness. He is seen to be God and none else. He is gladly confessed as the Lord of might. Luther's cry 'Let God be God!' is universal.

Thus man fulfils his chief end, which is to praise God and
glorify Him for ever. He turns from the false worship of
his own achievements and acknowledges that the Lord
alone is worthy of all honour. The prophet Isaiah complained that in a period of backsliding the children of
Israel had lapsed into materialistic idolatry. 'Their land
also is full of silver and gold, neither is there any end of
their treasures; their land is also full of horses, neither is
there any end of their chariots. Their land also is full of
idols; they worship the work of their own hands, that
which their own fingers have made: and the mean man
boweth down, and the great man humbleth himself'
(Isaiah 2. 7-9). What is the remedy? It is to recognise
the sovereignty of God. 'Enter into the rock, and hide
thee in the dust, for the fear of the Lord, and for the glory
of His majesty. The lofty looks of man shall be humbled,
and the haughtiness of men shall be bowed down, and
the Lord alone shall be exalted in that day' (Isaiah 2.
10-11).

This paramount purpose of revival is reflected in the
records of every Pentecostal season. In his attestation of
the Cambuslang awakening William McCulloch is
careful to ascribe glory to God lest it should be thought
that the detailed account he supplies was in any way
attributable to human causes. 'Need I guard against
having it supposed that in speaking of what happened
here in 1742 I am forgetting that it was all of God—of
free sovereign grace? The speakers were but as the rams'
horns in overthrowing the walls of Jericho. The power is
not in their words—it flowed through them. It is His to
bear the glory whose temple the soul is when prepared by
His grace and Spirit.' And again at the close McCulloch
writes: 'Upon the whole I think I may say "The Lord
hath done great things for us whereof we are glad." To
Him alone be all the glory and praise of whatever good

was got or done in that remarkable work of His grace.'

In the Skye revival of 1812-1814 the sense of God's overruling majesty was strongly felt. Donald Munro and the other leaders we read were continually filled with adoring wonder. 'That it was the Lord's doing, not man's, soon became so evident that they were made to feel, and exulted to acknowledge, that they were not to be accounted of and not worthy to be named in connection with the glorious manifestation which it pleased the Most High to vouchsafe of His redeeming love. "What are we and what is our Father's house?" was the language of their hearts while they contemplated the effects of the irresistible power now savingly exerted.'

The Welsh awakening of 1859 was characterised by a similar recognition. One note seemed to swell above the rest: that God had done all things well and was worthy to receive honour and glory and blessing. It is abundantly apparent in this report on the outbreak of revival in a Carmarthenshire town. 'One Sunday morning, an elder rose to speak, and his first remark was that the God they worshipped was without beginning and without end. "Amen!" exclaimed a young girl in the highest notes of a lovely voice, 'Blessed be His name for ever.' This cry might be compared to the touch of the electric button that shivers a quarry into a thousand hurtling fragments. Scores leapt from their seats, and, gathering in the vacant space in the centre, they gave vent to their pent-up emotions in outcries that were almost agonising in their ardour and intensity.' Again and again in J. J. Morgan's account of the '59 revival in Wales the recurrence of such a storm of praise is noted. The same trait may be traced throughout the 1904 awakening. It was much more a time of prayer and praise than of preaching. Unless the glory of God was uppermost no blessing ensued. Often Evan Roberts refused to speak until the spirit of glad adoration was released. On one occasion at Llansamlet he sat with his face buried in his hands because of the coldness of the meeting. Half an hour passed and then a young woman broke the ice with prayer 'People have come here ' she said 'to see the man and not the Master.' This brought the missioner to his feet. Pale and trembling with emotion, he rebuked the congregation for failing to put God first. 'One might think that you had come here from the North Pole,' he told them, 'but if you had passed Calvary you would be warmer than you are. You have been expecting me to rise for some time, but I could not. You have placed man before God. Is it not right for the creature to give obedience to the Creator? Is it not right that the saved should yield to the Saviour?'

Since the purpose of revival is the revealing of God's grace, it is not surprising that all the great movements of the Spirit have been accompanied by an outburst of sacred song. That is the natural expression of praise. The Reformation set all Germany singing Luther's hymns. Methodism was born in song and the eighteenth century saw the birth of a new musical impulse amongst the people of God. The Welsh revivals were each marked by *moliannu* which was a joint chorus of rapturous praise from preacher and congregation together. In the 1859 awakening both in Britain and America sacred music played a major part and the Gospel singer found an abiding place beside the Gospel preacher. Thus it is that in times of renewal the people of God glorify His grace.

The purpose of revival is also THE REJOICING OF GOD'S PEOPLE. Its upward intention is the glory of God, but its inward aim is to encourage the Church. A season of clear shining always cheers it after rain. Then the priests are clothed with righteousness and the saints shout for joy (Psalm 132. 9).

Every period of spiritual renascence is marked by

rejoicing. In the eighth chapter of Acts we read how 'Philip went down to the city of Samaria and preached Christ unto them' (Acts 8. 5). This was the first place outside the Holy City to feel the impact of Pentecost. The inhabitants were unanimous in their attentiveness to the message of the evangelist. Not only were they impressed by the Word spoken but also by the Word acted as many were healed of their diseases. Large numbers believed and were baptised. The Holy Spirit was imparted to them. And what was the condition of Samaria after this revival had taken place? Verse eight informs us: 'And there was great joy in that city.' That is always the purpose and effect of God's re-creative activity.

It emerges when souls are liberated from the law of sin and death and imbued with the Spirit of life in Christ Jesus. Revival brings the joy of emancipation. 'With confession of sin, and the realisation of cleansing,' writes F. W. Hoffman in a volume published in the United States of America, 'the heart turns to God in a new and joyous faith. Christ is now recognised as the all-sufficient Saviour. The agony and darkness of guilt is past, and the soul is flooded with a deep and overflowing joy, a joy with which no earthly joy can compare, the joy of restored and unbroken fellowship with God.' But such joy is also related to the transformation that has taken place within the Church. The contrast between what was and what is cannot but produce a sense of spiritual elation. William Cooper, assistant to Benjamin Colman at Brattle Street Church in Boston, thus eulogises the effects of the New England revival. 'But what a dead and barren time has it now been, for a great while, with all the Churches of the Reformation! The golden showers have been restrained; the influences of the Spirit suspended; and the consequence has been, that the Gospel has not had any eminent success: conversions have been rare and dubious; few sons and daughters have been born to God; and the hearts of Christians not so quickened, warmed and refreshed under the ordinances, as they have been. . . . And now—behold! The Lord whom we have sought, has suddenly come to His temple. The dispensation of grace we are now under, is certainly such as neither we nor our fathers have seen; and in some circumstances so wonderful, that I believe there has not been the like since the extraordinary pouring out of the Spirit immediately after our Lord's Ascension. The apostolical times seem to have returned upon us: such a display has there been of the power and grace of the Divine Spirit in the assemblies of His people, and such testimonies has He given to the Word of the Gospel.' God's chosen cannot but rejoice when such a change is seen. They echo the Psalmist: 'Thou, O God, didst send a plentiful rain, whereby Thou didst confirm Thine inheritance, when it was weary' (Psalm 68. 9). Revival removes the reproach that covers the Church and must necessarily result in rejoicing.

'Some people criticise this joy,' said Evan Roberts once, at Maesteg. 'Let them criticise,' someone interrupted. 'I don't care, so long as we have a share in this joy.' 'Yes,' the evangelist continued, 'but they say the House of God is holy! Well, is not heaven holy? If there is joy in heaven, why should we not share it? Jesus is joyful because He, looking down, sees the work of His love going on, when Jesus rejoices we rejoice! The only danger in the midst of this joy is that we may forget the unsaved.'

That leads us directly to the last consideration raised by this portion of Psalm 85. The purpose of revival is THE RECALLING OF GOD'S EXILES. Its outward aim is to reach all who are still strangers to the knowledge of Christ. Mercy and salvation, mentioned together in verse 7, are not reserved for the favoured few but extended to the godless multitude. It is our Father's gracious will that all should be restored to fellowship with Himself. To this end He is ever seeking to win back the lost to the fold. 'Neither doth God respect any person: yet doth He devise means, that His banished be not expelled from Him' (2 Samuel 14. 14).

In a time of revival it would seem that the Almighty brings exceptional glory to His own name by converting the most notorious sinners to Himself through the conviction of the Spirit and the blood of the Cross. The most obstinate sceptic and the bitterest scoffer prove vulnerable to the weapons of this warfare. Charles G. Finney, often called the father of modern revivalists, was himself an instance of this overpowering grace. He tells us in his Memoirs that as a young man he was almost as ignorant of religion as a heathen. He had been brought up in the backwoods of America and had never even read the Bible until he was learning to be a lawyer. He was the despair of the Christians where he lived and encouraged others in unbelief. 'If religion is true,' mockers said to the faithful, 'why don't you convert Finney? If you can do that, we will believe in religion.' But Finney was apparently inconvertible. Yet prayers were constantly offered for his salvation and at last, without the employment of any human agency whatsoever, Finney was brought to Christ in the solitude of the woods as he pondered that word from Jeremiah 29. 13—'And ye shall seek Me, and find Me, when ye shall search for Me with all your heart.' As all the world knows now, his conversion touched off a revival that spread throughout the town of Adams and the surrounding area and had repercussions far beyond New York State or even America itself. It seemed that in planning to bring many sons to glory through the fire of revival God chose Finney as a kind of first-fruits of redeeming love.

The effect of one conversion upon another sets up a spiritual chain reaction which runs to remarkable lengths. The rapid spread of revival is largely due to this recurring factor. One of the most sensational events of the 1858 awakening in America was the regeneration of Orville Gardner, a boxing star who was better known as 'Awful' Gardner. He was so widely popular that his public testimony had an unusual effect upon those who moved in his sporting circles. Within a very short space several thousand had been swept into the kingdom, many of them profligate sinners. That has proved to be God's method again and again in revival. He blazes the trail, so to speak, by delivering some conspicuous figure from the bondage of sin and then using that miracle of grace to influence many more. Such is the strategy of Divine compassion in recalling His exiles.

It is at this point that the true relationship between revival and evangelism is clarified. In a genuine Pentecost the one is swallowed up in the other. When the tide of conversion begins to flow the normal techniques of soul winning become superfluous. One loving heart kindles another. Each new-born creature witnesses to the saving power of Christ and so the harvest is increased. All are carried away as with a flood and the Spirit does His own unhindered work. Surely this is the experience for which the pining Church must pray. If we long to see the multitudes brought to the Saviour it is for revival we must plead. Nothing less will restore God's banished ones to Himself. Let us pray with Isaiah, 'Oh that Thou wouldest rend the heavens, that Thou wouldest come down, that the mountains might flow down at Thy presence, as when the melting fire burneth, the fire causeth the waters to boil, to make Thy name known to Thine adversaries, that the nations may tremble at Thy presence! When Thou didst terrible things which we looked not for, Thou camest down, the mountains flowed down at Thy presence. For since the beginning of the world men have not heard, nor perceived by the ear, neither hath the eye seen, O God, beside Thee, what He hath prepared for him that waiteth for Him' (Isaiah 64. 1-4).

This, then, is the high purpose of revival. In its upward aspect—God's praise: in its inward aspect—our rejoicing: in its outward aspect—the sinner's salvation. Wherever there is real awakening these objectives will be abundantly realised. God does not fall short of His aim. He does as He says. If, therefore, His people unite to pray for a blessed shower, they will not be disappointed. When Habakkuk cried, 'O Lord, revive Thy work in the midst of the years, in the midst of the years make known; in wrath remember mercy' (Habakkuk 3. 2) he did not lift up his voice in vain. The Lord answered his impassioned petition and in vouchsafing revival He fulfilled His own purpose. 'God came from Teman, and the Holy One from Mount Paran. His glory covered the heavens, and the earth was full of His praise' (Habakkuk 3. 3).

CHAPTER X

THE MESSAGE OF REVIVAL

*'Finally, brethren, pray for us, that the Word of the Lord may
have free course, and be glorified, even as it is with you.'*
—2 Thessalonians 3. 1

THIS earnest request of the apostle Paul contains a
glowing picture of the way in which the Word of God
dominates the spiritual scene in a time of revival. It
enjoys a sovereign liberty. Nothing can hinder it. It
spreads like an uncontrollable forest fire. When God
chooses to refresh His people with a season of spiritual
renewal, 'He sendeth forth His commandment upon
earth: His Word runneth very swiftly' (Psalm 147. 15).
Paul sees the message of revival speeding on to gain new
victories throughout the world and he longs that his own
ministry may share in the untrammelled blessings of the
Spirit. So he covets the prayers of the Thessalonian
Christians in order that with him as with them this
authoritative life-giving Word 'may have free course
and be glorified.' Bishop Lightfoot translated that
phrase as 'have a triumphant career.' The expression is
intended to suggest the omnipotence of the Gospel. It is
indeed 'the power of God unto salvation to every one
that believeth; to the Jew first and also to the Greek'
(Romans 1. 16). Linked with the explosive dynamic of
the Word is the uninhibited autonomy it always exercises.
It is a law unto itself. No man can tame it. Comments
Professor William Neil: 'The Word of the Lord is spoken
of as if it were almost an independent spiritual force
sweeping through the country under its own impetus,
and not relying on the eloquence and physical powers of

the missionaries.' That is why the citizens of Thessalonica received it so gladly, 'not as the word of men, but as it is in truth, the Word of God, which effectually worketh in you that believe' (1 Thessalonians 2. 13).

This verse epitomises the function of the Word in revival. It wins its widening way. It fulfils God's behest. 'So shall My Word be that goeth forth out of My mouth: it shall not return unto Me void, but it shall accomplish that which I please, and it shall prosper in the thing whereto I sent it' (Isaiah 55. 11). The consequence is that it is glorified. It proves its own power and grace and brings honour to God's great name. When Paul and Barnabas declared the Word to the Gentiles at Antioch, 'they were glad, and glorified the Word of the Lord: and as many as were ordained to eternal life believed' (Acts 13. 48).

Every revival in history has been marked by a similar pre-eminence of the Word. Blessing can only accrue as the Gospel goes from victory unto victory. A scrutiny of the evidence in Acts will show that in the Pentecostal awakening all the glory of success is ascribed to this cause. 'And the Word of God increased; and the number of the disciples multiplied in Jerusalem greatly; and a great company of the priests were obedient to the faith' (Acts 6. 7). 'But the Word of God grew and multiplied' (Acts 12. 24). 'And this continued by the space of two years; so that all they which dwelt in Asia heard the Word of the Lord Jesus, both Jews and Greeks. . . . So mightily grew the Word of God and prevailed' (Acts 19. 10, 20). Pentecost provides the pattern of all genuine revival and we are not therefore surprised to discover that this selfsame feature is stamped upon the successive quickenings of the Church in subsequent centuries. The Protestant Reformation was essentially a return to the Word and a renascence of preaching. The Puritan movement in

England focussed upon the ministry of exposition and popularised what were known as 'prophesyings' or meetings to hear the message of the Lord. The Methodist revival of the eighteenth century was largely promoted through the preaching of the Wesleys and Whitefield. It may be said that revivals thrive on the Word and the Word is exalted in revivals.

If this be so, then the phenomenon of revival presents an inescapable challenge to preachers, whether clerical or lay. Pentecost must needs pass through the pulpit. There can be no short-circuit which leaves the messenger of God untouched. Unless the Gospel trumpet is lifted to his lips, no gracious visitation will ensue. Hence we need to realise afresh with Finney that 'all ministers should be revival ministers, and all preaching should be revival preaching.' The note of expectancy must be recaptured. Preachers must concentrate upon this single objective. If they truly long for revival they will preach so as to make Christians go home and pray and sinners go home and weep. Unless the stewards of God's mysteries desire and fervently anticipate the shower of blessing, it is not likely to fall upon their hearers.

What, then, is the nature of the revival message? What are the grand characteristics of Pentecostal preaching? Let us enumerate them one by one. First, the message of revival is GOD-GLORYING. The flying angel of the Apocalypse appointed to preach the everlasting Gospel 'unto them that dwell on the earth, and to every nation, and kindred, and tongue and people' (Revelation 14. 6) in the latter days, proclaims the theme of all effective preaching. 'Fear God, and give glory to Him; for the hour of His judgment is come: and worship Him that made heaven, and earth, and the sea, and the fountains of waters' (Revelation 14. 7). That is the primary accent of the revival message. It magnifies the supreme excellences of Almighty God and calls on men to adore their Maker by submitting to the Lordship of Christ and the Leadership of the Holy Spirit. It must not be forgotten that the Gospel, as first announced by the angelic host, began with the anthem, 'Glory to God in the highest . . .' (Luke 2. 14).

An examination of the homiletical literature pertaining to the major periods of revival within the Church of Christ reveals that this emphasis upon God's glorious sovereignty is universal. Sermons that have exhibited the nature, attributes and works of the triune Godhead have been most frequently and unmistakably attended with regenerating grace. 'This kind of preaching is many a time the thunder and lightning that remove the stagnation, miasma, and the oppressive heat that before pervaded the moral atmosphere, and are followed by a cool, bracing, and refreshing breeze from the presence of the Lord,' according to G. W. Hervey, who adds a number of instances in the chapter of his *Manual of Revivals* from which the above quotation was extracted.

But not only must the sermon aim at the glory of God: the preacher himself must have no other end in view. Such deliverance from the snares of men-pleasing is only accomplished by the sanctification of the Spirit. In his searching address on 'The Duty of a Gospel Minister,' first proclaimed in the High Church Yard of Glasgow in 1741, George Whitefield told a story which doubtless did not miss its mark. A presbytery of ministers was being addressed by one of their number. In the course of his utterance he supposed that the Last Judgment had come and that the Lord Jesus Christ was upon the throne of His authority and calling His ministers to account. He asked one of them, 'What did you preach for?' He replied, 'Lord, there was a patronage in the family of £150 a year; I therefore took orders to get the presentation.' 'Stand thou by,' said the Lord, 'verily thou hast thy reward.' He asked another, 'What did you preach for?' And he said, 'I preached that I might be reckoned a fine orator, and to have applause of men.' 'Stand thou by,' said the Lord, 'verily thou hast thy reward.' A third was likewise asked, 'And what did you preach for?' 'Lord, Thou knowest my heart,' was the response, 'I did not seek to please men; and though many infirmities have passed in my ministry, I did it with an upright design to promote Thy glory.' The Lord Jesus immediately cried out, 'Make room, angels, for this My dear servant. Thou hast honoured Me on earth; sit here by Me on My throne.'

The message of revival is BIBLE-BASED. It never strays beyond the Book. It accepts the Holy Scriptures as given by inspiration of God and as containing all things necessary for salvation. What has been described as the reverential approach to the revealed Word has typified all great revival preaching. When God is looking for a mouthpiece, His concern is not to locate the exceptionally eloquent or the prodigiously learned. He can best employ the man who is ready to receive with meekness the ingrafted word. Not that intellectual superiority is regarded as a hindrance; it only becomes so when it sets itself up against the wisdom of God. Men of outstanding mental capacity like John Calvin, Jonathan Edwards, John Wesley, and Thomas Chalmers were signally used of God when they laid their reasonings at His feet. 'To this man will I look,' says the Lord, 'even to him that is poor and of a contrite spirit, and trembleth at My Word' (Isaiah 66. 2).

A Bible-based ministry will inevitably produce doctrinal preaching. Despite the current aversion from dogmatism of any sort, there can be no room for disagreement with the claim that any spiritual recuperation must be accompanied by a return to sound doctrine. 'As I turn my eyes backward upon a prolonged and varied ministry, nothing impresses me more deeply than the importance of doctrine,' declared Dr. Dinsdale T. Young towards the close of his days. 'No feature of the Church's life evokes my alarm so much as the too general depreciation of doctrine. It is a sinister sign. . . . It still remains true that it is dogmatic Christianity which wins men and renews and affords them power to serve their generation, and furnishes them with peace and joy, and radiant hope.' Whether men will hear or whether they will forbear, this is the type of preaching which flourishes under revival and under which revival flourishes. Shortly after Dr. R. W. Dale was settled in the pastorate of Carr's Lane Congregational Church in Birmingham, he was accosted in the street by a fellow-minister. He said, 'I hear that you are preaching doctrinal sermons to the congregation at Carr's Lane; they will not stand it.' Dale simply answered. 'They will have to stand it.' Such must be the determination of every Gospel messenger. For, as David Matthews has rightly affirmed, 'orthodox theology has always proved to be the hidden source of true revival.'

The limits of this present chapter do not permit a detailed review of the salient items of the evangelical message so inseparable from the re-enactment of Pentecost. A letter from John Newton's *Cardiphonia* will suffice to indicate something of its scope. It contains a kind of creed, which is still worth noting. 'I believe that sin is the most hateful thing in the world; that I and all men are by nature in a state of wrath and depravity, utterly unable to sustain the penalty or fulfil the commands of God's Holy Law; and that we have no sufficiency of ourselves to think a good thought. I believe that Jesus Christ is the chief among ten thousand; that He came into the world to save the chief of sinners, by making a propitiation for sin by His death, by paying a perfect obedience to the law on our behalf, and that He is now exalted on high to give repentance and remission of sins to all that believe; and that He ever liveth to make intercession for us. I believe that the Holy Spirit (the gift of God through Jesus Christ), is the sure and only guide into all truth, and the common privilege of all believers; and under His influence, I believe the Holy Scriptures are able to make us wise unto salvation, and to furnish us thoroughly for every good work. I believe that love to God, and to man for God's sake, is the essence of religion and the fulfilling of the law; that without holiness no man shall see the Lord; that those who, by a patient course of well-doing, seek glory, honour, and immortality, shall receive eternal life; and I believe that this reward is not of debt, but of grace, even to the praise and glory of that grace whereby He has made us accepted in the Beloved.' When such is the tenour of faithful preaching, blessing cannot be long withheld.

The message of revival is CHRIST-CENTRED. It honours the Father by exalting the Son. It sets the Saviour in the foreground of the picture. It points away from all else to Him. It declares with Peter, 'Neither is there salvation in any other: for there is none other name under heaven given among men, whereby we must be saved' (Acts 4. 12). Said Whitefield in the sermon already mentioned: 'It is not the business of the ministers of the Gospel merely to entertain people with harangues of dry morality, and leave out Jesus Christ. It is not our business to entertain our people, as Cicero, Seneca, and other heathen moralists did; but we are to preach Christ, not ourselves; we are to preach the hidden mysteries of the Kingdom.'

This concentration upon Christ has always been a distinctive feature of Spirit-filled preaching. It was so on the day of Pentecost. After Peter had announced his text from the prophecy of Joel, the opening statement of his sermon was this: 'Jesus of Nazareth, a man approved of God among you by miracles and wonders and signs which God did by Him in the midst of you, as ye yourselves also know; Him, being delivered by the determinate counsel and foreknowledge of God, ye have taken, and by wicked hands have crucified and slain: Whom God hath raised up, having loosed the pains of death: because it was not possible that He should be holden of it' (Acts 2. 22-24). And again in his speech at the Beautiful Gate of the Temple Peter declared: 'The God of Abraham, and of Isaac, and of Jacob, the God of our fathers, hath glorified His Son Jesus; whom ye delivered up, and denied Him in the presence of Pilate, when He was determined to let Him go. But ye denied the Holy One and the Just, and desired a murderer to be released unto you; and killed the Prince of life, Whom God hath raised from the dead; whereof we are witnesses' (Acts 3. 13-15). When Paul reminds the Corinthians how he delivered to them as of first importance that which he had already received, his rehearsal of basic Gospel truths consists entirely of facts about the fact of Christ: 'How that Christ died for our sins according to the Scriptures; and that He was buried, and that He rose again the third day according to the Scriptures' (1 Corinthians 15. 3, 4). When John speaks of the message which he and his companions have heard from God and declared to their hearers, he says that it concerns the Lord Jesus Christ, who is 'the Word of life' (1 John 1. 1). Christ, then, is the focal centre of the earliest Christian preaching. As Bishop Barry has put it: 'The good news that thundered across the Roman Empire and brought back hope to a disillusioned world was not prescriptions about Christian conduct: it was "Jesus and the Resurrection".'

'Behold the Lamb of God which, taketh away the sin of the world' (John 1. 29): that has always been the core of the revival message. 'We preach always Christ and Christ alone, true God and true man,' exclaimed Luther; 'that may seem a limited and monotonous subject, likely to be soon exhausted, but we are never at the end of it.' 'In Him is the whole stuff of our salvation,' stated Calvin. 'I never got away from Jesus Christ and Him crucified,' confided Brainerd, concerning his methods with the Red Indians. 'I have only one sermon,' declared Höfacker, 'Come, sinners, and look on Christ!' 'I build my study on Mount Calvary,' affirmed Spurgeon. 'I have tried to preach Jesus Christ,' claimed Alexander Maclaren. With one accord the company of preachers unites to testify that Christ crucified and risen is the central theme of the saving message. Said William Burns of Kilsyth, 'While prayer, as we have seen, is the spirit of a revival of religion, the substance of a revival—the pillar and ground of all is the sound, zealous, pointed preaching of Christ—the compliance with the command, "Go, stand, and speak unto the people of all the words of this life' (Acts 5. 20)".'

The message of revival is SOUL-SAVING. It is directed towards the goal of conversion. The salvation of the hearer is the motive of the preacher. The Gospel bow is not drawn at a venture. The sights are set on the target from the start. In a season of awakening what the French call 'the preaching of conquest' will prevail. Samuel Rutherford told his congregation, 'My witness is above, that your heaven would be two heavens to me, and the salvation of you as two salvations to me.' One of Thomas Chalmers's parishioners recalled that 'he would bend over the pulpit and press us to take the gift as if he held it at that moment in his hand, and could not be satisfied till everyone of us got possession of it.' A simple Scotswoman said of Robert Murray McCheyne, 'He preached as if he was dyin' a'most to have ye converted' and Andrew Bonar testified concerning him that 'he was insatiably greedy of souls.' In every sermon that Spurgeon delivered, it was claimed, there was a plain path of salvation for the penitent sinner.

Henry Ward Beecher admitted that he had prepared and preached hundreds of sermons before he realised what is the real design of the pulpit. For a long time preaching with him was an end in itself, but when he received the fulness of the Spirit he saw that it was only a means. 'Then it appeared a definite, practical thing,' he said. 'Preaching was a method of enforcing truths, not for the sake of the truths themselves, but for the result to be sought in men. A sermon was good that had power on the heart; and was good for nothing—no matter how good—that had no moral power on man.' The message of revival is always ready to submit to such a test. It aims at a verdict and is not satisfied until it has gained one.

Soul-saving preaching will be directed against sin; it will not shrink from presenting the challenge of the law; it will warn of judgment to come and the eternal punishment of the impenitent; it will dwell much on the wounds of Jesus and the efficacy of His atoning blood; it will speak of so great salvation purchased for all who will believe and receive. And it will not stop short of a specific application, a simple offer and an earnest appeal. Even an unsympathetic critic like Benjamin Kennicott could not fail to feel the force of this feature of John Wesley's preaching. 'Then he came to what he called his plain, practical application. Here was what he had been preparing for all along.' That is what every preacher must aim at from the start. Only such preaching will befit revival. May every messenger of the Lord be given what Dr. Scofield called 'a fresh dip in Jordan' to be ready for God's hour!

CHAPTER XI

THE AGENT OF REVIVAL

*'Ye shall receive power, after that the Holy Ghost is come
upon you: and ye shall be witnesses unto Me both in Jerusalem,
and in all Judaea, and in Samaria, and unto the uttermost part
of the earth.'*   —Acts 1. 8

ONE of the most valuable and interesting books which
has ever come into my hands comprises a set of
lectures on revivals of religion given by Dr. William B.
Sprague. They were originally delivered to his own
congregation at the Second Presbyterian Church in
Albany, New York State, and constitute one of the
classical contributions to the literature on this subject.
They were first published in the year 1832. But here in
my temporary possession, on loan from the Evangelical
Library, is the author's signed presentation copy to none
other than Charles Simeon, the great Christian leader in
the latter years of the eighteenth and the beginning of the
nineteenth centuries, whose influence extended far beyond
the Cambridge parish of which he was vicar. Underneath
the inscription 'The Rev. C. Simeon, with great regard
from W. B. Sprague' is added Simeon's own testimony to
the usefulness of the volume. 'A most valuable book. I
recommend my executor to keep it; as there are few, if
any, others in this kingdom. I love the good sense of
Dr. Sprague. C.S.'

We shall introduce our chapter on the agent of revival
by adopting a helpful distinction drawn by Sprague in his
fourth lecture. He states categorically that God is the
grand author of spiritual regeneration, whether in the
individual believer or in the Church as a whole, but that

He works in a twofold manner. The first agency is that of providence. God orders all things according to the counsel of His will. He has a plan which includes all events and embraces even the numbering of hairs and the falling of sparrows. There are no accidents in His universe. Nothing ever happens in the life of any person which does not answer some purpose in the chain of Divine superintendence. This is nowhere more apparent than in the events which lead up to conversion. But if God so overrules what we are pleased to describe as circumstance in order to achieve the salvation of a single believer, it is not surprising to learn that He does so on a much larger scale to pave the pathway to revival. Behind every great awakening we can trace the mysterious hand of providence clearing the trail of blessing. God often uses catastrophe to drive men to Himself. 'Calamity,' said Sir William Davenant, 'is the perfect glass wherein we truly see and know ourselves.' And when men are brought to recognise themselves as they really are, then God can begin to impress upon their hearts the need of redemption. So it was in the very period when the seventeenth century Poet Laureate gave utterance to the dictum quoted above. The Plague of London in 1665 swept the city from end to end and mowed down thousands of victims. Dreadful as it was, this scourge was the means of bringing many face to face with God and proved to be the instrument of a genuine revival of faith. It was here that the Puritan movement flowered into an awakening and so, as J. R. Green observed, 'it was from the moment of its seeming fall that its real victory began.' Now that the sword was sheathed, the spiritual work for which the Puritans stood went on and prospered in a most remarkable manner. Sinners were turned from their vanities to the living and true God, and believers were stirred to the pursuit of holiness. Ministers of the Gospel were sought for from all quarters—they were regarded as the most essential members of the community. When death trod the streets of London in 1665, life was lived from a fresh angle because the time was short. The gracious intervention of providence through tragedy was plain for all to see.

But if this be the general and indirect agency of God in producing revival, His specific and direct mode of operation is through the Holy Spirit. The Third Person of the Trinity has been designated from eternity to perform this function. The Son firmly promised that the Father would send the Spirit for this very end. That assurance was reiterated before our Lord ascended to the right hand of God. 'Ye shall receive power,' He told the apostles, 'after that the Holy Ghost is come upon you.' There could be no spiritual reinvigoration without Pentecost. The gift of the Spirit brought with it the abiding possibility of revival. The Comforter was installed as the permanent Administrator of the Church. Something occurred at Pentecost which is altogether unique. The Holy Spirit was bestowed not as a transient guest but as a settled resident. 'And I will pray the Father,' said our Lord, 'and He shall give you another Comforter, that He may abide with you for ever' (John 14. 16). That prayer was answered at the first Whitsuntide.

> 'Our glorified Head, His Spirit hath shed,
>   With His people to stay,
>   And never again will He take Him away.'

The Holy Ghost is given to the Church as the perpetual agent of revival. In one sense, Pentecost can never happen again. In another sense, it may always be happening since we live in the age of the Spirit. 'Nothing can be more directly contrary to the intention and teaching of the Word than to expect 'a second Pentecost.' I would as soon look for a second Calvary,' wrote Dr. J. Elder

Cumming. 'But this does not imply that the experience of the disciples at Pentecost is not to be known again. On the contrary, it is because the Spirit, who then began His special work, is still present in the Church to continue it, that Pentecost admits of no repetition. Whether the miraculous results may once more be seen in the later days of the Church yet to come, we know not certainly; though the Book of Revelation seems to lead us to expect this. But the spiritual results have continued, in greater or less measure, and among more or fewer of the people of God; and they are to be looked for, desired, asked, and by faith attained.' The once-for-all bestowal of the Spirit to the Church at Pentecost implies the potentiality of continuous revival. God will never remove the Holy Spirit from us, but we may grieve Him and resist His influence (cf. Ephesians 4. 30; Acts 7. 51).

The agency of the Spirit in revival may be considered from several angles. He is revealed in Scripture as THE CONVICTING SPIRIT. Our Lord clearly recognised this feature of the Paraclete. 'And when He is come, He will reprove the world of sin, and of righteousness, and of judgment; of sin, because they believe not on Me; of righteousness, because I go to My Father, and ye see Me no more; of judgment, because the prince of this world is judged' (John 16. 8-10). This was the effect of the Holy Spirit at Pentecost, when we learn that after Peter's preaching, 'they were pricked in their heart, and said unto Peter and to the rest of the apostles, Men and brethren what shall we do?' (Acts 2. 37). A similar response was evoked in the case of the Philippian gaoler who cried out, 'Sirs, what must I do to be saved?' (Acts 16. 30).

This is the initial role of the Spirit in revival. Only He can unlock the sinner's heart and bring illumination and conviction. 'The natural man receiveth not the things of the Spirit of God: for they are foolishness unto him: neither can he know them, because they are spiritually discerned' (1 Corinthians 2. 14). The Holy Ghost begins by lighting up the mind and conscience so that sin can be seen in all its sordid ugliness. And sin is unbelief. 'If ye believe not that I am He,' said our Saviour, 'ye shall die in your sins' (John 8. 24). That is the essence of iniquity —to believe in the ego as the great I am, and to reject Christ. As Dr. Vincent Taylor has neatly expressed it, sin is self-coronation. It means that man usurps the throne that belongs only to the King of Kings. The Holy Spirit convicts of such wilful pride.

Then He proceeds to convince the unbeliever about the reality of righteousness. The overwhelming disclosure of sin might well drive to despair did not the Comforter immediately reveal that Christ by His death, resurrection and ascension had opened up the highway of holiness for even the worst of offenders. His perfect righteousness is available and adequate to transform the vilest. And the Holy Spirit further assures that this righteousness will ultimately prevail. Indeed, it has already conquered, for 'the prince of this world is judged' (John 16. 10). 'There is therefore now no condemnation to them which are in Christ Jesus' (Romans 8. 1)—that is the glad consequence for the believer. But for those who spurn the Saviour's call, judgment has begun already and at the last they will be 'punished with everlasting destruction from the presence of the Lord, and from the glory of His power, when He shall come to be glorified in His saints, and to be admired in all them that believe' (2 Thessalonians 1. 9, 10). Without this threefold conviction regeneration cannot take place. That is why it is the first work of the Spirit in a time of revival.

Scripture has more to tell us about the agency of the

Spirit. It reveals that He is THE QUICKENING SPIRIT. He is the Lord and Giver of Life. All life is due to His activity. He is its medium and originator. 'The Spirit is life' (Romans 8. 10) and therefore 'the Spirit giveth life' (2 Corinthians 3. 6). He is properly designated 'the Spirit of life' (Romans 8. 2). His distinctive work is regeneration. It is He who implants the seed of new spiritual existence. 'Except a man be born of water and of the Spirit, he cannot enter into the kingdom of God' (John 3. 5).

In a season of revival the Holy Spirit conducts a dual mission. He quickens sinners so that they are reborn in Christ and He quickens believers so that they walk in Him. This latter is as vital as the former. Indeed, as Finney used to say, Christians are more to blame for not being revived than sinners are for not being converted. Believers have already received the Spirit and, having tasted His sweet influence, they should long for His fulness. Revival is often arrested because God's people resist the Spirit. They are unwilling to let Him quicken them into the holiness that it is His function to impart. This double operation of the Holy Ghost is intended to produce awakening both in the sinner and in the slumbering saint.

Quickening is of the essence of revival. The very meaning of the word indicates the association. Hence it is clear that the Holy Spirit must needs be the supreme agent of revival, since it is His prerogative to dispense fresh life. All the vigour and vitality so evident in a time of renewal is derived from this Divine source. The transformation of the Church is directly due to the animation of the Spirit. Wrote Samuel Chadwick, 'The Spirit giveth Life, and the Spirit working through the Life strengthens, directs and transforms. He reveals the Face of Christ, and transforms into the same image, from glory to glory, even as from the Lord the Spirit. All understanding of the Truth as Truth is in Jesus, is by the Lord and Giver of Life Who spake by the prophets, and is given to guide believers into all the Truth. All Christ-likeness of life and character is by the transforming power of Life through the Spirit of the Living God, the Lord and Giver of Life. That is why the work of God in the Church depends upon the Life of the Church. The City of the Living God comes through the Spirit of the Living God. That is why an ecclesiastical dignitary may know less about conversion than a Hallelujah lass of the Salvation Army! That is why spiritual power is so often in inverse ratio to scholastic accomplishments! It is not by might of carnal strength, nor in the power of organised authority, but by the Spirit of the Lord. Life is greater than all the resources of natural power.'

Such is the quickening we need today. Let this then be our universal prayer.

'O Breath of Life, come sweeping through us,
Revive Thy Church with life and power;
O Breath of Life, come, cleanse, renew us,
And fit Thy Church to meet this hour.'

But this is not all that God's Word teaches concerning the agency of the Spirit. It reveals that He is THE ENABLING SPIRIT. He is the bringer of power. He is power and He supplies power. 'Ye shall receive power,' promised our Lord, 'after that the Holy Ghost is come upon you.' And again in Luke 24. 49: 'Tarry ye in the city of Jerusalem until ye be endued with power from on high.' The Spirit is the gift of power.

Notice that it is a gift to be received. Spiritual power is not something that is created by man. It is conferred by God. It comes from above and not from below. It is humbly accepted, not proudly acquired. Man cannot snatch or steal this gift of gifts from the hand of God. He must wait on the Lord and acknowledge that as the promise is His so the blessing is His also. That is most noticeable in the verse which concerns us just now. 'After that' is all important: it reminds us of the interval between the confession of our own inadequacy and the demonstration of God's enablement.

With equal clarity this same passage points to the Holy Spirit as the provider of power. Indeed, He *is* the power He Himself conveys. Enduement with power is the mark of His presence. His name of Comforter bears witness to His nature. He is the Strengthener, the Enabler, the Empowerer. The English rendering of the title Paraclete as Comforter is misleading since it suggests to the average reader that the ministry of the Holy Spirit is primarily one of solace and soothing. The strict derivation from the Latin *cum fortis*—with strength—ought to dispel any such notion. The Spirit is the One who comes to our side when we are sinking and lifts us up. He puts new energy into us. He imparts power. It is He alone who enables the believer and the Church.

The most familiar of Zechariah's eight visions is recorded in the Fourth Chapter of his prophecy. He is shown the golden lamp that stands in the Temple. It has seven branches. Its seven lamps are fed by seven pipes from a bowl which stands above them. Two olive trees on either side maintain a living supply to the reservoir. Mystified, as well he might be, by this strange device, Zechariah asks his angelic companion, 'What are these, my Lord?' (Zechariah 4. 4). And the angel replies in words that are graven upon our hearts for ever: 'Not by might, nor by power, but by My Spirit, saith the Lord of hosts' (v. 6). 'Who art thou, O great mountain?' the message continues. 'Before Zerubbabel thou shalt become a plain: and he shall bring forth the headstone thereof with shoutings, crying, Grace, grace unto it' (v. 7).

There were many obstacles in the path that led to the erection of the Second Temple after the exile. But the Word of the Lord assured that they would all be triumphantly overcome. The hill of difficulty would be reduced to a level plain. The final coping-stone of the entire fabric would be brought out and set in its place amidst the applause and admiration of the people, as they exclaimed how beautiful it was. And all this—here is the deep significance of the vision—all this would be accomplished, not by human means or ingenuity, not by might or power of earth, but by the Holy Spirit. His would be the work and His alone. He only is the Enabler. That is the lesson we still need to learn. No one else can provide power save the Holy Ghost.

One thing more we read in Scripture with respect to the agency of the Spirit. It reveals that He is THE CONTROLLING SPIRIT. He is the Governor of the Church. He is in supreme command over all its administration. He is the true Vicar of Christ and He guarantees that all shall be ordered in accordance with the Father's will. That is why genuine revival will never run amok. It will certainly get out of human hands, but it will never elude the Divine control.

The Spirit created the Church as the body of Christ. Prior to Pentecost the apostles were a conglomeration of assorted units, but the baptism of fire welded them into a corporate entity. This was the living organism which the Spirit was to indwell and activate. When Christ came to earth He assumed our flesh and tabernacled with us. For the Holy Spirit there was no such incarnation, as Oswald Sanders reminds us in a telling paragraph. The mystical Body of Christ became His vehicle of expression. Within that sphere He reigns and governs with absolute authority. A study of Acts confirms this conception of the relationship between the Spirit and the Church. Every aspect of the worship and witness of the primitive Christian community was directly controlled by the Paraclete. Christ Himself had assured the disciples that the Comforter would lead them into all truth (John 16. 13) and henceforth all decisions were referred to Him. At the Council of Jerusalem a disputed matter of faith and practice was settled under His supervision and in the resultant epistolary address to the Gentiles in Antioch, Syria and Cilicia this astonishing formula is found: 'For it seemed good to the Holy Ghost, and to us . . .' (Acts 15. 28). The appointment of officers within the Church is entirely within the jurisdiction of the Spirit. In his farewell to the Ephesian elders Paul urges them to take heed 'to all the flock, over the which the Holy Ghost hath made you overseers, to feed the Church of God, which He hath purchased with His own blood' (Acts 20. 28). Those who are chosen to fill even the subsidiary offices within the Christian society must be men 'full of the Holy Ghost' (Acts 6. 3). And when there is urgent missionary work to be undertaken, we read that the Holy Ghost Himself took the initiative and said, 'Separate Me Barnabas and Saul for the work whereunto I have called them' (Acts 13. 2). The Spirit also guides and upholds God's servants in their ministry and equips them to preach the Gospel with due effect.

This oversight of the Spirit is the safeguard of revival against extravagances. 'God is not the author of confusion, but of peace, as in all the churches of the saints' (1 Corinthians 14. 33). Wherefore, even in the midst of Pentecostal manifestations, all things will be done decently and in order (v. 40). Revival is always in danger of lapsing into its counterfeit and thus undoing the work of God, but wherever the Spirit is Lord no licence will be mingled with liberty. Many sincere misgivings with regard to revival would be allayed if this necessary factor of the Spirit's control were taken fully into account. When He leads we need not fear to follow.

The Spirit's agency in revival has its outcome in widespread blessing. From Jerusalem the initial impetus of Pentecost stemmed out in ever broadening circles through Judaea and Samaria to the uttermost part of the earth. It was the harbinger of that era of universal quickening which is forecast in the Word before the Lord returns May we see its glorious dawn even in our troubled time!

CHAPTER XII

THE TIDE OF REVIVAL

*'Therefore being by the right hand of God exalted, and
having received of the Father the promise of the Holy Ghost,
He hath shed forth this, which ye now see and hear.'*

—Acts 2. 33

THIS verse from Holy Writ enshrines the interpretation of Pentecost disclosed by the revealing Spirit
to the apostle Peter. It comes from the first Christian
sermon ever preached and was uttered under inspiration
from above. The fearless fisherman flung out an uncompromising challenge to the very men who had brought
the Lord Jesus to the Cross. God he declared had
overturned their infamous verdict on His Son. The
prince of life, whom they had crucified and slain, had
been raised up by the power of the Almighty and now
sat at the right hand of the heavenly majesty. More than
that: having received from God the long-awaited promise
of the Holy Spirit, He has poured out this, which they
see and hear. So far from being safely put away, as they
supposed, in the finality of the tomb, the same Jesus was
behind all these amazing manifestations of Pentecost. The
Jews thought they had done with Him, but He had not
done with them. He—the despised Nazarene whom they
had nailed to the cruel tree—had shed forth this.

The precedents of Pentecost are of the utmost significance. Only because the Lord Jesus has been exalted
has the Spirit been vouchsafed. Only because the Lord
Jesus was raised from the dead could He be exalted. And
only because the Lord Jesus died for our sins could He
be resurrected for our justification. Pentecost is thus the

complement of Calvary. Just as the Jewish feast of the fiftieth day depended on the Passover so Whitsuntide is related to Good Friday. The saving Cross, the empty tomb, the heavenly throne and the tongues of fire are all links in a golden chain. They serve to emphasise the intimate connection that still exists between Christ and His Church. Though absent from earth in the body of flesh, which resides at God's right hand and not here (as the last rubric of the Holy Communion in the Book of Common Prayer so rightly insists), our Lord is ever at hand in His spiritual presence through the ministry of the Comforter, whose office it is to make Christ real to His own.

It is the tendency of our contemporary generation to evade the challenge of Christ. Times have moved on, it is said. This is the twentieth century and we have outgrown the need for a Saviour. He was suitable for the pre-scientific age, but not for ours. We are children of the atomic era: He is far too old-fashioned to help us and so we can conveniently forget Him. But it is not nearly so easy as such people imagine to dispose of the Lord Jesus. We cannot escape Him so simply. He haunts us. He has a habit of coming back at us just when we think we have banished Him, as the Jews of the New Testament period discovered. In all the evidences today of the Holy Spirit's activity throughout the world—and they are many and considerable—we are confronted with the living, reigning Christ. *He* has shed forth this, which we now see and hear. Revival is the Saviour's manifestation of His presence through the agency of the Spirit in fulfilment of the Father's purpose. Wherever it breaks out it is stamped by the marks of Christ. That is why Professor James S. Stewart has claimed that 'revival is a new discovery of Jesus.'

But now let us turn from the Lord Jesus Christ who is

behind all 'this, which ye now see and hear' and enquire precisely what 'this' was and is. 'He hath shed forth this.' God had lifted Jesus to heaven and the risen, ascended Saviour had poured out the Holy Spirit upon His followers. That gift, as we have already seen, spelt power. New resources became available for those discouraged disciples. They were liberated from fear, they were delivered from doubt, they were equipped with abundant energy, they were filled with unshakeable assurance. The Spirit was come. It was an experience which transformed those previously defeatist apostles into men who turned the world upside down (Acts 17. 6). From being weak, vacillating, pusillanimous, they became strong, certain and daring.

An experience which can effect such an astonishing revolution in the lives of ordinary men must have been real enough. And it was. But how to express it, how to explain it to others—there was the rub. It broke through language and escaped. It was too big to define with any sort of adequacy. Words failed. Only poetic analogies could even begin to do justice to the truth. And so the Scripture resorts to symbols as it seeks to convey to our restricted finite minds the amplitude and irresistibility of the Spirit's action. The first symbol is wind: 'And suddenly there came a sound from heaven as of a rushing mighty wind, and it filled all the house where they were sitting' (Acts 2. 2). The next is fire: 'And there appeared unto them cloven tongues like as of fire, and it sat upon each of them' (v. 3). And now in verse 33 we meet a third. The Holy Spirit is shed forth. That conjures up a vivid picture of the boundless and relentless ocean as it flows towards the shore. The Holy Spirit is here presented to our minds under the analogy of the tide.

The verb employed by Peter often recurs in the New Testament to denote different kinds of pouring. It is

used in Matthew 9. 17 with reference to the decanting of
wine. In John 2. 15 it describes how our Lord when
cleansing the Temple overthrew the tables of the money
changers and poured out their coins in a veritable stream
on to the floor. In Acts 1. 18 it appears in a rather grue-
some medical context at the suicide of Judas, when we
are told that 'all his bowels gushed out.' In Revelation
it alludes to the emptying of the vials of God's wrath
upon the earth (Revelation 16. 1-4). Best of all, this verb
is dyed in Calvary red as our Lord takes the cup at the
Last Supper and tells His disciples, 'This is My blood of
the new testament, which is shed for many for the
remission of sins' (Matthew 26. 28).

The selfsame term is more than once applied to the
Holy Spirit, and in each case would seem to suggest the
tide of revival. In Acts 2. 17, 18, where Peter is citing the
prophecy of Joel, it is twice repeated. 'And it shall come
to pass in the last days, saith God, that I will *pour out* of
My Spirit upon all flesh: and your sons and your daughters
shall prophesy, and your young men shall see visions,
and your old men shall dream dreams: and on My
servants and on My handmaidens I will *pour out* in those
days of My Spirit; and they shall prophesy.' The literal
exactitude of Scripture is evidenced in the fact that in
the verse before us in Acts 2. 33 Peter adheres to the
precise Greek verb as is found in the Septuagint version
of Joel 2. 28, 29. Again in Acts 10. 45 the same word
appears in a different form to denote the manner in
which the Spirit fell on all who heard Peter speak at
Caesarea. 'And they of the circumcision which believed
were astonished, as many as came with Peter, because
that on the Gentiles also was *poured out* the gift of the Holy
Ghost.' Titus 3. 6 speaks of the renewing of the Holy
Ghost 'which He (i.e. 'God our Saviour' v. 4) *shed* on us
abundantly through Jesus Christ our Saviour' and once

again the identical verb recurs. And finally in Romans 5. 5 we read of 'the love of God (which) is *shed abroad* in our hearts by the Holy Ghost which is given unto us.' All these passages unite to depict the tide of revival.

It is further delineated as something which can be both seen and heard. That is an accurate account of the surging sea. The eye is fascinated by the restless waves and the ear is assailed by the ceaseless roar. Pentecost was similarly impressed upon the senses of those who were present. They saw great signs and wonders and heard every man speak in his own language. Revival always makes its impact upon both Eye Gate and Ear Gate. It compels attention. It cannot be hid.

Let us, then, draw out a little more fully the analogy of the tide in relation to the work of the Spirit in revival. First of all, THE TIDE INVADES. It is alien to the land. It comes from without. It is an intruder. The tide represents a power from outside which invades the coast. Never, perhaps, in modern times was the essential otherness of the sea realised in these islands as in the dreadful winter of 1953. Those seaside towns on the Eastern shore of Great Britain which suffered so severely from the ravages of mighty waters felt that they were indeed being invaded by an intrusive force. A thoroughly foreign element was interfering with their peaceful lives.

The tide of the Spirit is like that. The Holy Ghost is an invader. He does not belong to this natural sphere. He is a supernatural being. He comes from over the border. His origin is in the great beyond. He breaks into the area of everyday existence from without. Despite all the restraints that men may erect to keep Him out He mows down every barrier and will have right of way. But although He is other than ourselves, the Holy Spirit is not hostile, save to sin. He has no malign intent towards our persons. He does not come to destroy anything but evil. His is a benevolent invasion. He comes to bring a blessing.

It is so fatally easy for men to grow completely preoccupied with the natural. We tend to dismiss the supernatural as unreal. We fail to recognise the nearness of spiritual irruption. At any moment all the forces of Pentecost may burst in upon us. But we are fools and slow of heart to believe. We shut our ears and hearts to the battering of the Spirit and so the tide takes us unawares. That is always the case in the world and all too often true of the Church as well. In *The Voyage* the late Charles Morgan made effective use of the figure of the harbour and the sea in order to illustrate this experience. He pictures the sort of mind which refuses to believe that the Holy Spirit can really make any impact on men's hearts and lives. He gives expression to this attitude through the conversation of some of his characters. One of them says, 'It's as if they were living in an enclosed harbour and had forgotten the sea outside. One day the sea flows in strongly; there is an exceptional tide and one says that "it's impossible", that it "isn't true", and the other throws up his hands and says—"It's a stroke of magic". Both forget the sea outside and that it is always there and always connected with the water in the harbour and some try to shut out the sea and pretend there is only the harbour. It is God's mercy that the sea breaks in or the water in the harbour would stagnate.' God's mercy: that is the nature of the Spirit's tide. He flows in to bless. Revival invades to stir the Church from fatal lethargy.

Then THE TIDE CLEANSES. It prevents putrefaction. It sweetens and purifies. It clears away all kinds of pollution. The slime and scum are carried far out to sea and lost in the mighty deep.

We know that from our visits to the seaside. On holiday at the coast we leave the beach at sundown after a full and happy day. Hundreds like ourselves have played and bathed and picnicked on the sands. The litter left behind would require an army of men to remove. But that army is not needed. When we go down to the shore next morning, God has been at work. Every scrap of rubbish has disappeared and the sands are smooth and clean. What has happened? The tide has been in and washed away the unsightly litter.

The tide of the Spirit is like that. The Holy Ghost always cleanses where He comes. He washes sinners in the laver of regeneration and makes them whiter than snow. Where He enters the heart He brings spotless purity. Revival and holiness are inseparable. Cleansing is God's will for each believer. And that cleansing can be complete. 'From all iniquity, from all, He shall my soul redeem.' The blood that was shed for all cleanses from all (1 John 1. 7). It is the Holy Spirit Who applies the benefits of Calvary to the heart. When the tide flows in, our iniquity is taken away and our sin is purged.

Revival is always a cleansing time. It purifies the soul of the believer and enables him to go on to perfection. It purifies the witness of the Church by removing everything that defiles, or works abomination, or makes a lie (Revelation 21. 27). It purifies the world around as the sweet and healing properties of the Spirit's flow dispel the poison of sin. Only eight months after he had begun his ministry amongst the colliers at Kingswood, Wesley could report that 'the scene is already changed. Kingswood does not now, as a year ago, resound with cursing and blasphemy. It is no more filled with drunkenness and uncleanness, and the idle diversions that naturally lead thereto. It is no longer full of wars and fightings, of clamour and bitterness, of wrath and envyings. Peace

E

and love are there. Great numbers of the people are mild, gentle, and easy to be entreated. They do not cry, neither strive, and rarely is their voice to be heard in the streets, or indeed in their own wood, unless when they are at their usual evening diversion—singing praise unto God their Saviour.' That is the invariable accompaniment of revival. Where the tide covers, it cleanses. Whenever the Spirit is bestowed, that happens. 'And God, which knoweth the hearts, bare them witness, giving them the Holy Ghost, even as He did unto us; and put no difference between us and them, purifying their hearts by faith' (Acts 15. 8, 9).

Again THE TIDE FILLS. Every tiny pool is replenished. Every channel is supplied. Nothing is overlooked. Nothing is left empty. The tide is thorough and inclusive. It fills every place. And it fills with all fulness. The plenitude of the boundless ocean is brought to the smallest bay. The most insignificant inlet receives all the treasures of the deep.

The tide of the Spirit is like that. The Holy Ghost fills. That is the distinctive verb to describe His coming. It is the very first to be used and it is the most suitable. 'And they were all filled with the Holy Ghost' (Acts 2. 4). That is the essence of Pentecost. That is the experience of revival. When the promise is fulfilled, believers are filled full. The deficiency in so many professing Christians is that they have not received the fulness of the Spirit. They may have been invaded. They may have been cleansed. But they are not yet filled. They have accepted some of what God has to give them in the Pentecostal provision, but not all. They have a measure, but not the overflowing amplitude. They have a taste, but not the satisfying cup. And the sad thing is that they are content with their low level of Christian living. They think they have the Spirit because they once made a profession of faith. They do not really want too big a dose of the Holy Ghost: they are afraid of where He might take them.

We are rightly sorry for those who suffer from lung trouble. When we hear of those who are living on one lung, or even half a lung, we wonder how they manage to keep going at all. The iron lung is a wonderful invention, but it makes us thankful that we do not need it. God has given us two sound lungs and we should be grateful with every breath we so freely draw. But there are people who are living spiritually on half a lung. They are gasping for breath. They find worship and witness and work in the Church far too much for them. They are always complaining that they have no time or strength for the commitments of the Christian life. And all the while they are trying to struggle on with only half a lung because they will not seek the fulness of the Spirit. God waits for them to take a deep breath and inhale all His sufficiency. His command is 'Be filled with the Spirit' (Ephesians 5. 18). In a period of revival the tide flows so strongly that the fulness floods many an empty soul that otherwise would have remained unblessed. And it pervades the congregation of the faithful before it captivates the whole community.

> 'It fills the Church of God; it fills
> The sinful world around.'

There are waters first to the ankles, then to the knees, next to the loins and finally the elevating swell of 'waters to swim in' (Ezekiel 47. 5).

Lastly, then, THE TIDE UPLIFTS. It bears on its broad bosom the great vessels which ply from shore to shore. And its strength can empower those that have been bereft of it. Some years ago a ship sank in the River Mersey. The wreck blocked the channel and prevented any ship from entering or leaving the port. Every effort to raise it proved vain. The tugs puffed and pulled in a fruitless endeavour to dislodge the derelict. Even the most massive and high powered cranes were futile. Then a young engineer had a brain wave. He suggested that at low tide barges should be attached to the hulk. His idea was quickly adopted. The waters began to rise and as the tide flowed in, the barges lifted, and with them the wreck that had caused so much inconvenience. Soon it was raised from its resting place and floated away.

The tide of the Spirit is like that. The Holy Ghost uplifts. He raises men and women to a higher plane. He enables them with a new and utterly surprising vitality. The Spirit is always associated with energy in the Word of God. He brooded over the chaos of the formless void at the beginning and brought it into order and under control. He was God's gift to man at his creation—the engine of his life, so to speak. Whenever in the Old Testament men were called by God to undertake special tasks and difficult commissions, they were equipped by the Holy Spirit. The prophets foresaw a time when the uplifting Spirit would be poured out upon all flesh and our Lord assured His followers that it would be so. At Pentecost both prophecy and promise were fulfilled. The tide of the Spirit flowed in and brought power to all. That is what repeatedly characterises revivals.

There can be no doubt that the one thing needful for the Church today is a fresh baptism in the tide of the Spirit. Such a Pentecostal flood would invade our human situation with a supernatural force that would cleanse and fill and uplift. O may it soon be granted! Our most urgent prayer should be that God will turn the tide and let the waters once more go out of Jerusalem.

CHAPTER XIII

THE FRUITS OF REVIVAL

'For I will pour water upon him that is thirsty, and floods upon the dry ground: I will pour My Spirit upon thy seed, and My blessing upon thine offspring: and they shall spring up as among the grass, as willows by the water courses. One shall say, I am the Lord's; and another shall call himself by the name of Jacob; and another shall subscribe with his hand unto the Lord, and surname himself by the name of Israel.'
—Isaiah 44. 3-5

IT is a common criticism of revivals to complain that they do not endure. The claim is confidently made that they are altogether evanescent. They simply come to pass and their permanent effect is negligible. Such a sweeping condemnation cannot be substantiated either from Scripture or history. It is, of course, sadly true that revivals have not maintained their peak of fervour over any lengthy span of years. There was even a descent from Pentecost. The conditions under which the apostle Paul laboured amongst the infant churches of Asia Minor and Eastern Europe were not continuously such as would be expected to obtain in the midst of an intense spiritual awakening. And so it has been ever since. There has been an observable ebb and flow of the tide in proportion to the prayer and faith of God's people. Had revival never suffered any diminution of power we should not be needing one today.

But to recognise the discontinuity of revival is a very different thing from bemoaning the unfruitfulness of such a season. These times of refreshing may come and go, but they certainly do not leave things just as they were, either in the Church or in the world. Their impact is

more than merely superficial. It penetrates below the
surface and exercises an unintermitting influence long
after the first fine careless rapture has departed. Revival
truly represents an advance in depth. That was what
impressed John Wesley as in 1777 he reviewed the course
of the Methodist awakening in his now celebrated
sermon at the Foundation of City Road Chapel, London.
Taking as his text Numbers 23. 23, 'What hath God
wrought?' he commented upon the extent and swiftness
of the movement. Then he proceeded to expatiate on its
lasting effects. 'We may likewise observe the depth of the
work so extensively and swiftly wrought. Multitudes have
been thoroughly convinced of sin; and, shortly after, so
filled with joy and love, that whether they were in the
body, or out of the body, they could hardly tell; and, in
the power of this love, they have trampled under foot
whatever the world accounts either terrible or desirable,
having evidenced, in the severest trials, an invariable and
tender goodwill to mankind, and all the fruits of holiness.
Now, so deep a repentance, so strong a faith, so fervent
love, and so unblemished holiness, wrought in so many
persons in so short a time, the world has not seen for
many ages.' And lest it be supposed that Wesley's own
judgment could hardly be altogether impartial, let us
add the considered statement of an accepted expert,
whose High Church views would be unlikely to pre-
dispose him towards a favourable estimate. This is the
verdict of Canon John H. Overton in his book on *The
Evangelical Revival of the Eighteenth Century*. 'Of the faith
which enabled a man to abandon the cherished habits of
a lifetime, and to go forth ready to spend and be spent in
his Master's service, which made the selfish man self-
denying, the discontented happy, the worldling spiritually-
minded, the drunkard sober, the sensual chaste, the liar
truthful, the proud humble, the godless godly, the

thriftless thrifty, we can only judge by the fruits which it bore. That such fruits were borne is surely undeniable.' A similar conclusion must be reached with respect to all the great revivals, if a genuinely objective approach is made to the available evidence.

Revivals, therefore, do not fear to meet to the Master's test, 'By their fruits ye shall know them' (Matthew 7. 20). Men do not gather grapes of thorns or figs of thistles. A corrupt tree cannot bring forth good fruit, any more than a good tree can bring forth evil fruit (v. 17). We are quite content to allow revival to be judged by its fruit. The nature of that fruit is symbolised in this poetic passage from Isaiah 44. When the Spirit has been poured forth in blessing, God's children will spring up like grass between the streams and as willows by the water courses. The Holy Spirit is the agent of both physical and moral renewal, and here the one is typified by the other. But not only will the stunted growth of Israel be quickened into new life and verdure: even those outside the chosen seed will be affected and seek the overflow of blessing. Men who formerly refused to recognise God will gladly acknowledge that they now belong to Him and are not ashamed of His name. Indeed, they are prepared to bear His mark upon them, as pagan devotees were branded with the sign of their deity. All this is the fruit of revival. And what we glean from history's page amply serves to confirm the Word of God. We have time only to touch and glance upon a few of the gracious consequences of the Spirit's presence.

Revival brings A NEW SENSITIVITY TO SIN. That is always a noticeable feature. Wherever there is a real and penetrating work of God it will be accompanied by a deepened conviction of sin. Backsliders are rebuked and unbelievers faced with the awful punishment that awaits their rejection of Christ. Men will be constrained to cry with Job, 'I abhor myself' (Job 42. 6); with Asaph, 'I was as a beast before Thee' (Psalm 73. 22); with Ephraim, 'I was ashamed, yea even confounded' (Jeremiah 31. 19); with the publican, 'God be merciful to me a sinner' (Luke 18. 13).

The records of revival are replete with instances. Here is Jonathan Edwards speaking out of his experience in Northampton, Massachusetts. 'Commonly the first thing that appears after men have been much awakened, is a conviction of the justice of God in their own condemnation, in a sense of their own exceeding sinfulness, and the vileness of all their performances.' Here is Halley of Muthill, in Scotland: 'All those with whom I conversed appeared to be touched to the quick—the arrows of the Almighty shot to their very hearts—trembling like the jailor, and crying out against sin.' Here is an army officer describing what he saw in Cellardyke, Fife, in 1860: 'Men who were thought to be, and who thought themselves to be, good, religious people . . . have been led to search into the foundation upon which they were resting, and have found all rotten, that they were self-satisfied, resting on their own goodness, and not upon Christ. Many turned from open sin to lives of holiness, some weeping for joy for sins forgiven.' Here is Duncan Campbell's account of revival on Berneray in the Hebrides. 'I came out of the church, and the Spirit of God swept in amongst the people on the road as a wind. They gripped each other's arms in terror and fear. In agony of soul they trembled before the presence of God. They wept, and some fell to the ground, under deep conviction of sin.' Such renewed sensitivity of conscience leads to a veritable avalanche of enquiries concerning the way of salvation and holiness. 'Godly sorrow for sin, universal hatred at it, renouncing their own righteousness, and embracing the righteousness of God by faith in

Jesus Christ, embracing Him in all His offices, universal reformation of life, a superlative love to the blessed Redeemer: these'—according to James Robe of Kilsyth —'are the happy fruits of this blessed work, and sufficiently demonstrate that it is of the operation of the Spirit of God.'

Revival brings A NEW CONSECRATION TO GOD. Holiness becomes the goal of God's children. They seek that righteousness which only Christ can impart. And as the graces of the Redeemer and the ninefold fruit of the Spirit appear in the lives of believers, the unregenerate are compelled to take notice of them that they have been with Jesus. 'Had we a man among us, that we could produce, that did live an exact Gospel life'; said Benjamin Whichcote, the first of the Cambridge Platonists, 'had we a man that was already gospelized; were the Gospel a life, a soul, and a spirit to him . . . he would be the most lovely and useful person under heaven. Christianity would be recommended to the world by his spirit and conversation.' What Whichcote wistfully longed to see actually happens in revival. Men and women are so renewed in the spirit of their mind that they 'put on the new man, which after God is created in righteousness and true holiness' (Ephesians 4. 24). The result is so startling that even the most cynical sceptic cannot gainsay it.

Testimonies to the reality and influence of this consecration to God are to be found in profusion in the annals of revival. And as one reads the thrilling evidence it becomes increasingly apparent that the righteousness that characterises the people of God in a day of awakening is of a strictly practical kind. Holiness is expressed in the world, not out of it. It is related to the stark challenge of everyday living. It is at this point that a genuine work of the Spirit is distinguished from its spurious counterpart. No mere emotional upheaval can produce the flowers of righteousness. Only a deep and vital movement of God's power can so transform the lives of sinful men and women. 'The fruit of the Spirit is in all goodness and righteousness and truth' (Ephesians 5. 9). The consequences of revival are to be observed in a new honesty, a new sobriety, a new reliability, a new probity. Business and commerce, industry and social life are all affected.

One instance amongst many must suffice. During the Lewis revival in the nineteenth century a serious famine reduced the islanders to sore straits. Many were on the verge of starvation. A ship, laden with meal, was driven upon the shore by a storm. There it lay, with its precious cargo inviting plunder. Twenty years beforehand the inhabitants of Lewis would have had no compunction in seizing the opportunity of unlawful loot, even without the added excuse of hunger. It would have been a case of each man for himself. But now it was different. 'Every portion was accurately weighed or divided,' says the narrative, 'and, as their necessities were so great that they had nothing then to pay, their affectionate minister gave a promissory note for it, knowing well that the excellent lady whose property the lands are, would not suffer him to be impoverished. The people knew this also, but none took advantage of it, all were occupied in economising to the utmost, till one after another they had repaid their debt. Thus they obtained not only the great blessing of necessary food, but preserved the still greater blessing of integrity, and a spirit free from covetousness.' In such down-to-earth ways as that revival reflects a fuller consecration to God bringing with it a loftier ethical standard. In the day of Pentecostal power the injunction of Micah 6. 6 assumes central significance. 'He hath shewed thee, O man, what is good; and what doth the Lord require of thee, but to do justly, and to love mercy, and to walk humbly with thy God?'

Revival brings A NEW LOYALTY TO THE CHURCH. A real work of the Holy Ghost always builds up the Body of Christ. It is His especial function to strengthen the assembly of the faithful. Converts are incorporated into the redeemed community by the operation of the Spirit. So Paul can tell the Gentile believers at Ephesus that they are no longer strangers and foreigners, but 'fellow citizens with the saints, and of the household of God,' resting upon Christ the sure foundation stone, 'in Whom all the building fitly framed together groweth unto an holy temple in the Lord; in Whom ye also are builded together for an habitation of God through the Spirit' (Ephesians 2. 21, 22). In Pentecostal seasons there are added unto the Church daily such as shall be saved.

Revival restores the sanctity of the Lord's Day. The Sabbath is no longer despised. It is remembered and hallowed according to the law of God. 'Instead of worldly and common discourse on the Lord's day, there is that which is spiritual and good to the use of edifying', said James Robe in his narrative of the Kilsyth awakening in 1742. 'There is little of what was formerly common, strolling about the fields, or sitting idle at the doors of their house on that holy day. There is a general desire after public ordinances.' The worship of God's house is given priority. The goings of God are seen in His sanctuary (Psalm 68. 24). 'Our public assemblies were beautiful,' wrote Jonathan Edwards. 'The congregation was alive in God's service; every one earnestly intent on the work; every hearer eager to drink in the Word; the assembly in general, from time to time, in tears; some weeping with sorrow and distress: others, with joy and love: and others, with pity and tender concern for the souls of their neighbours.' During the ministry of Samuel Walker, the Anglican Evangelical, in Truro in mid-eighteenth century it was said that 'you might fire a cannon down every street in Church time without a chance of killing a human being.' The appetite for God's Word is immeasurably sharpened during a time of revival. The Bible becomes a new Book since the Interpreter Spirit opens up its meaning. 'Their love for the Scriptures was great,' reported Dr. John Hamilton, of the Barony Church, Glasgow, with reference to the Cambuslang converts. 'They spoke of them as very precious, and as an invaluable treasure. They seemed surprised how they could have so slighted them before, and they wondered at the discoveries which they were daily making in them.' When George Whitefield preached to Ralph Erskine's congregation at Dunfermline he encountered a pleasing circumstance which he recorded in his journal. 'After I had done prayer, and named my text, the rustling made by opening the Bibles all at once quite surprised me; a scene I never was witness to before.' When revival at length struck the moribund flock at Middleborough, Massachusetts, which had wellnigh broken Peter Thacher's tender heart, the pastor was able to testify with joy: 'From this time, there was an un-common teachableness among my people: scarce one word of counsel seemed lost, or a sermon in vain. From this time they must have four sermons in a week, two Tuesdays, two Thursdays: the Word of the Lord was very precious in those days.'

Devotion to the ordinances of the Church and especially to the sacrament of the Lord's Supper is a further feature of this new ecclesiastical loyalty. Many of the notable movements of the Spirit in Scotland were associated with the solemn Communion seasons. In Wales, it was at Whit-sun celebration in Talgarth Church that Howell Harris was converted in 1735. The Methodist movement from the start was sacramental as well as evangelical, and the Wesleys saw many souls brought to Christ at the table of the Lord's appointing. The camp meetings of America, which were so mightily beneficial in periods of spiritual ardour, were originally convened to prepare for the reception of the Holy Communion. Wherever revival spreads, the Lord's Supper is recognised as a real means of grace and a Love Feast which anticipates by faith the heavenly banquet in the age to come.

Revival brings A NEW LOVE OF THE BRETHREN. All are one in Christ Jesus. 'Names, and sects and parties fall' and believers of every persuasion are united in their common Lord. The Spirit Himself effects the true ecumenical integration. 'It is gloriously impossible for those who are reconciled to God in Christ Jesus,' wrote John Bonar in a glowing passage, 'to be permanently unreconciled to one another, and a time of revival, bringing out all the great realities in which they are at one, and sinking all the minor points on which they are divided, has a blessed tendency to unite their hearts, and so gradually to unite their hands in the work of the Lord. O it is sweet to see how in such a time the holy of all sects and denominations are invincibly drawn together by the constraining influence of the "love of the Spirit." It is sweet to find that the divided and separated Body of Christ is yet one. It is sweet to discover, beneath the rents at which the world has so long mocked, cords of love still, which bind them fast together by binding them all to one great centre, and that centre Christ.' That is precisely what we are led to expect when the Spirit is at work, for His fruit is 'love, joy, peace, long-suffering, gentleness, goodness, faith, meekness, temperance' (Galatians 5. 22, 23). In the Pentecostal era 'the multitude of them that believed were of one heart and of one soul' (Acts 4. 32) and a similar unity is apparent in every hour of revival.

'Till the Revival came,' wrote Professor William

Gibson concerning the 1859 Awakening in Ireland, 'we had no conception of such a social state as is described by Luke "And they, continuing daily with one accord in the temple, and breaking bread from house to house, did eat their meat with gladness and singleness of heart, praising God and having favour with all the people" (Acts 2. 46, 47). But we can now in some measure understand it. The difficulty now is, not to bring the people to the sanctuary, but to induce them to retire from its cherished precincts; an abounding and pervasive joy manifesting itself in open-hearted hospitality, and welcome given to the brethren in Christ; the very countenance irradiated as by a beam of heavenly glory; the everyday life a psalm of praise; and the adorning of the doctrine of God our Saviour so palpable and attractive as to win all hearts, constraining even the impenitent to accord the tribute of esteem and admiration. These are the indications of a higher tone and a holier brotherhood than have generally been exemplified in the Church.' Not only does revival bring unity within the local church but also between the various Christian bodies. 'In the Awakening of 1858,' says Dr. J. Edwin Orr, 'the various denominations were so busy trying to cater for the influx of new members that there was no room for sectarian jealousy. With scarcely an exception, the churches were working as one man. Arminian and Calvinist ignored their differences; Baptists and Paedobaptists were blessed together; and everything was lovely, almost too good to be true. By common consent, doctrinal controversies were left alone, and the idea worked well. At last the world was able to say, without irony, "Behold, how these Christians love one another"!' At a great mass meeting on August 22, 1860, during the Perthshire revival, the sponsors declared that they 'buried sectarianism in the South Inch of Perth that day, and saw no Christian weep over its grave.' That is always the effect of revival. It promotes a new love of the brethren.

Revival brings A NEW CONCERN FOR THE LOST. It rekindles the passion for souls. It stimulates the zeal to win others for Christ. It provides evangelism with a cutting edge. 'We cannot but speak the things which we have seen and heard' protested Peter and John (Acts 4. 20). In a season of spiritual refreshment that same urge impels every believer. 'We are journeying unto the place of which the Lord said, I will give it you: come thou with us, and we will do thee good' (Numbers 10. 29): that is the invitation on the Christian's lips.

The lost can never be won by remote control. The Church must go out and fetch them. Revival supplies a powerful new dynamic which drives believers out into the highways and hedges to compel the wanderers to come in. The message of salvation is taken to the people where they are—in the streets, in the fields, in their homes, in the workshops, in the public houses. The records of revival reveal that this passion for the lost knows no bounds and overcomes all barriers. At all costs the Gospel must be brought to those who need it most, wherever they may be. That is why the awakenings of the Spirit have invariably stimulated missionary enthusiasm. Not content that the good news should be spread at home, men in whom the fire of Pentecost burns have felt the need to send the Word to the uttermost parts of the earth. That is why it has been said that every revival in the homelands is felt within a decade on the foreign field. The Baptist Missionary Society, the London Missionary Society, the Church Missionary Society and the Methodist Missionary Society were all born out of the Evangelical revival of the eighteenth century. The first parallel organisation in America, the Board of Commissioners for Foreign Missions, was founded in 1810 as a result of the conversion of Samuel J. Mills in the 1800 awakening. The singular work of the Spirit amongst the Moravians at Herrnhut in 1727 inaugurated a missionary undertaking which extended to the far places of the world and antedated by more than half a century the more general interest of Protestantism in the propagation of the Gospel in distant lands. Nor must it be forgotten that the Religious Tract Society and the British and Foreign Bible Society were both the products of revival.

This concern for the lost does not confine itself to the salvation of souls, but extends to the welfare of the whole man. Revival rouses the social conscience and leads to the removal of injustices and the amelioration of living and working conditions. It encourages the care of the sick, the orphan and the widow, the prisoner and the pauper. 'Is not this the fast that I have chosen? to loose the bands of wickedness, to undo the heavy burdens, and to let the oppressed go free, and that ye break every yoke?' (Isaiah 58. 6). Revival gave birth to the Sunday School movement, the abolition of slavery, the relief of the poor, the reform of prisons, the passing of factory acts and the provision of orphanages. Those who pin their faith in merely humanitarian reform, and who airily and inaccurately dismiss the fruits of revival as being only of a spiritual nature, should reconsider the facts and revise their hastily formed opinion. The evidence for the far-reaching social effects of Pentecostal quickening has been patiently amassed and impressively presented by recent researchers. It has long been realised that the movement of the Spirit in eighteenth century England profoundly influenced the life of the nation at every level, and, in the view of W. E. H. Lecky, spared our green and pleasant land the horrors of the French Revolution. Now Dr. J. Edwin Orr has provided parallel documentation for the following century both in Britain and America. With reference to the eighteenth century, Richard Niebuhr has declared that America 'cannot eradicate, if it would, the marks left upon its social memory, upon its institutions and habits, by an awakening to God that was simultaneous with its awakening to national self-consciousness.' Timothy L. Smith has written at length about *Revival and Social Reform in Mid-Nineteenth Century America* and elucidated the largely overlooked relationship between evangelical Protestantism and the rising tide of philanthropic concern. When God moves in to bless He does not ignore His needy children's cry. He fills His Church with a new burden for the lost and sends out His ambassadors to bring deliverance both from the bondage of sin and the bondage of oppression.

These, then, are the undeniable fruits of revival. 'Such tremendous results are the justification of revivals,' says Ernest Baker. 'When we speak of praying and working for revival now, we have not in mind the creation of a wave of religious emotion only, but the availing ourselves of the tremendous moral and spiritual forces which God offers to men, and by means of which permanent additions will be made to the religious, social and philanthropic life of the world.' Let us never allow our vision of revival to be narrowed within any preconceived limits. The Spirit waits to do a work in our midst which will once again turn the world upside down. May He have free course in our hearts and, in the day of God's determination, renew the earth in righteousness.

F

CHAPTER XIV

THE MYSTERY OF REVIVAL

'The wind bloweth where it listeth, and thou hearest the sound thereof, but canst not tell whence it cometh, and whither it goeth: so is everyone that is born of the Spirit.' —John 3. 8

ONE of Scotland's outstanding sons was Dr. Alexander Whyte. Preacher, statesman, scholar, saint, he bestrid the narrow ecclesiastical world of his time like a Colossus. He was indeed a mighty man of God. His fame has gone out into all the earth, but what is not so often recognised is that he was the spiritual child of a great revival. As a student he was caught up in the swelling tide of the 1859 awakening which flooded the heathered Highlands. Young Alexander Whyte entered into a deeper religious experience and tasted the joy and assurance of full salvation as a result of this association. His preaching gained a new and vital note and, as his biographer, Dr. G. F. Barbour, points out, the two marks of the revival which recur constantly in the reminiscences of its survivors—a profound sense of sin and an intense experience of the power of prayer—became and remained the most distinctive features of Dr. Whyte's own message. Fifty years later, addressing a commemoration gathering, Alexander Whyte, then Principal of New College, Edinburgh, declared: 'A revival quickens dead men, touches men's imaginations and sets loose their hearts. . . . There is a Divine mystery about revivals. God's sovereignty is in them. Just when His time comes, "a nation shall be born in a day," and it gives us a heart of hope to think of that. It is in His hand. "Thou hast ascended up on high: Thou hast led captivity captive." And Thou hast the Holy Ghost to give to Thy Church and people.

I may not live to see it. But the day will come when there will be a great revival over the whole earth.'

Now that is the mighty hope which sustains the faithful in this generation as in the last. In a season of spiritual barrenness, when the Church is in what John Wesley called 'the wilderness state,' we wait for the consolation of Israel. We rejoice in the signs of the times which encourage us to believe that our redemption draws nigh. But we know also that revival is not yet. So we tarry the leisure of the Lord. We watch and pray, we toil and sing, but we realise that revival will arrive in God's good time, not at our beckoning. We cannot create or compel a revival. We can only receive it. That is the Divine mystery of this phenomenon.

A word in our Lord's conversation with Nicodemus in the familiar Third Chapter of the Gospel according to John takes us right to the heart of this pregnant truth. Verse eight contains a miniature parable of the Spirit. Our Saviour refers Nicodemus to the analogy of the wind. Perhaps as they sat together, either inside the house, or even on the flat roof top, the wind began to rise and disturb the stillness. It rustled amongst the trees and sighed around the streets. It picked up dead leaves and odd bits of rubbish and sent them scampering away. 'Listen, Nicodemus, to the wind! It is free to blow wherever it likes. You can hear its sound, as you do just now, but you cannot tell where it has come from or where it is going. The new birth is like that. It is a mystery of the Spirit.' Now what being born again is to the individual, revival is to the Church. Regeneration is the revival of a man and revival is the regeneration of a community. We shall therefore expect the analogy of regeneration to hold good for the miracle of revival, and we shall be right, for both are the work of the Holy Ghost. 'It looks as though there were seasons in the course of history,' wrote Rufus Jones in *The Eternal Gospel*, 'which are like vernal equinoxes of the Spirit when fresh initiations into more life occur, when new installations of life seem to break in and enlarge the empire of man's Divine estate.' Such outbreaks are aptly named revivals and we may profitably enquire into the nature of their mystery.

It is, as Dr. Whyte observed, a mystery related to God's sovereignty. 'Verily Thou art a God that hidest Thyself, O God of Israel, the Saviour' (Isaiah 45. 15). The Almighty is under obligation to no man to explain Himself. 'He giveth not account of any of His matters' (Job 33. 13). His judgments are a great deep. 'Thy way is in the sea, and Thy path in the great waters, and Thy footsteps are not known' (Psalm 77. 19). Shall any therefore teach God knowledge or enjoin Him His way? 'Who hath directed the Spirit of the Lord, or being His counsellor hath taught Him? With whom took He counsel, and who instructed Him, and taught Him in the path of judgment, and taught Him knowledge, and showed to Him the way of understanding?' (Isaiah 40. 13, 14). All His purposes are veiled from our sight, unless He graciously chooses to disclose them, and are hidden in the Sinai mists that swathe His sovereign holiness. Mystery is an adjunct of His majesty, and 'it is the glory of God to conceal a thing' (Proverbs 25. 2). Revival falls within the category of secret things which belong to God alone. Only as He condescends to reveal His will through His deeds are we permitted to gain a glimpse of His unsearchable ways. Mystery, then, is of the very essence of revival. If it were otherwise, it would not be the work of God.

REVIVAL IS MYSTERIOUS IN ITS ORIGIN. It is like the wind. We cannot tell whence it comes. The movements of the wind are invisible and untraceable. We may observe the weather vane and conclude, 'It is a west wind from the sea,' or, 'It is a north wind from the hills,' but we know not what glens, what moors, what mountains, what cities, what hamlets it has passed before it fanned our cheeks. We know not in what frozen snows or tropical haze the breeze has had its birth. Its origin is wrapped in mystery.

So it is with revival. We have no adequate instrument to plot its course. Consequently it springs upon the wondering Church unheralded and unexpected. 'The origins of all great movements in history are shrouded in darkness,' remarked Canon L. E. Elliott-Binns, 'and religious revivals in particular have a habit of breaking out suddenly and almost unaccountably.' 'Suddenty' is a rare legal term to denote an act of God which is so totally unlooked for and unpredictable that normal claims for insurance cannot be pressed. There are 'suddenties' in the spiritual realm, as an examination of the incidence of the adverb 'suddenly' in Scripture will show, and the most notable of all as it affects us today is revival. Pentecost itself was just such an occurrence, and so is every renewal of that initial outflow of the Spirit. 'And *suddenly* there came a sound from heaven as of a rushing mighty wind. . . .' (Acts 2. 2). The wind rises without warning. The element of surprise is never absent from revival. Even believers who have yearned and prayed for blessing are taken joyfully unawares by the swift answer to their pleadings, and unbelievers are shaken to their unsound roots. At Pentecost we are told that 'they were all amazed and marvelled' (v. 7) and again, 'they were all amazed, and were in doubt' (v. 12). That is continually God's way. He strikes when none but the faithful are in the least suspecting that He may intervene and even they are ignorant of the times and seasons of His mighty saving acts. 'I have declared the former things from the beginning; and they went forth out of My mouth, and I shewed them; I did them *suddenly*, and they came to pass' (Isaiah 48. 3)

Revival presupposes the decline of the Church and it is therefore consistent with its nature that it should be manifested out of the midst of depression and decay. That God's quickening power should burst forth upon such an unpropitious scene is altogether surprising to those who experience it and only serves to deepen the mystery. 'The revivals of Christianity have occurred when the funeral of the faith seemed nigh' says Baker. They have represented a fresh inrush of life into a body which is in danger of decease. The resuscitation of the doomed and dying patient is clearly seen to be a miracle of Divine origin. None but God Himself could so re-energise a moribund Church.

Few could have guessed on the eve of the Protestant Reformation that the gates of new life were to swing open so soon to the troubled world. The institutional Church had reached the nadir of corruption. Papal tyranny was at its extreme. The curia was notorious for its immorality and love of luxury. The monasteries were in sore need of reform and the local clergy were largely blind leaders of the blind. The crass materialism which had gripped the whole hierarchial system was epitomised in the campaign to popularise indulgences. Yet it was in the midst of such unlikely circumstances that God was about to bless His people with revival. No wonder the pious remnant rejoiced, 'for the thing was done suddenly' (2 Chronicles 29. 36).

The Evangelical revival in England in the eighteenth century was preceded by what Balleine has dubbed the 'Glacial Epoch' in the Anglican Church. The poet Southey acknowledged that 'there never was less religious feeling, either within the Established Church, or without, than when Wesley blew his trumpet, and awakened those who slept.' Sir William Blackstone, the distinguished jurist, was sufficiently curious, early in the reign of George III, to go from church to church and hear every clergyman of note in London. He reported that he did not hear a single discourse which had more Christianity in it than the writings of Cicero, and that it would have been impossible for him to discover, from what he heard, whether the preacher were a follower of Confucius, of Mahomet or of Christ. Bishop Butler complained that 'it is come, I know not how, to be taken for granted, by many persons, that Christianity is not so much as a subject of enquiry, but that it is now at length discovered to be fictitious. And, accordingly, they treat it as if, in the present age, this were an agreed point among all people of discernment, and nothing remained but to set it up as a principal subject of mirth and ridicule, as it were by way of reprisals, for its having so long interrupted the pleasures of the world.' It was in such a day that God chose to bare His arm and make known His majesty. 'The wind came from heaven,' wrote Dr. John S. Simon, 'it blew where it listed, its sound was heard in the towns and villages of England, and under its influence the deadly mists were dispersed, the veiled heavens were cleared, a new spring day of fresh, full, more abundant life shone about the people, who, having walked in darkness, saw a great light.'

The mysterious origin of revival is amply substantiated by an appeal to history. Accessions of new power occur when every hope seems dimmed. Of a truth, the end of man's tether is the beginning of God's deliverance. Even amid the atomic gloom of our uncertain age it may be that He is preparing to bless if the few are faithful. All the more reason, then, for us to be much on our knees and about the King's business, lest the day of refreshing should find us unready.

REVIVAL IS MYSTERIOUS IN ITS OPERATION. The continuation is with God as well as the inception. It is like the wind. It blows where it lists. We may tell the direction of the breeze that tinges our cheeks with colour. We can devise instruments to measure its velocity. We can watch its effect as it ripples the golden corn or causes the trees to clap their hands together. But we cannot control it. We cannot cramp its freedom. We cannot alter its invisible track.

That is a parable of the Spirit's working. 'You cannot restrict the action of the Divine Breath, or prescribe its course, any more than you can dictate to the winds of heaven,' declared Professor H. B. Swete in his definitive study of New Testament Pneumatology. 'That the wind is at work we know by familiar sounds of breeze or gale, but its origin and destination are hidden from us. Such is the manner of the Spirit's working in him who has been born from above; there is the same mystery surrounding it, the same ignorance on man's part of the laws by which it is governed, the same certainty that its existence and its presence are matters of fact, since its effects fall within our range of observation, even within the cognizance of the senses; the Spirit's voice is heard in human utterances, though the Spirit itself is inaudible and invisible.' As in regeneration, so it is in revival. The Holy Ghost is not confined in His operation by any man-made rule. He breathes as and where He will. We cannot forecast the pattern of revival. 'God moves in a mysterious way His wonders to perform.' The next great spiritual awakening may be utterly unlike any that has gone before. We must beware, then, of an undue fixity in our conception of revival. The Holy Spirit is not limited to a stereotype. He enjoys and exhibits an untrammelled liberty.

That is reflected in His selection of instruments. The Holy Spirit expresses Himself through the most unlikely

channels at times. He is like the wind, and the wind is
no respecter of persons. Huw Menai, the poet, saw that
when he wrote about 'The Happy Vagrant.'

> 'To that strenuous democrat
> The Wind, I doff my battered hat,
> Who asks no permit of His Grace
> The Duke to blow upon his face.'

With the impartiality and unpredictability of the wind
the Holy Spirit directs the work of revival. Sometimes
He chooses for His vessels the strong and the wise. Sometimes He picks out the weak and the simple. But always
He carries on His revitalising project and imparts the
breath of new life to the pining Church. By no means
all the human vehicles of revival have been illustrious
and renowned. Many more have been obscure and
endowed with but one talent. Who, for instance, has
heard of Samuel Buell? And yet even though still
unordained and only a few months out of college, he was
remarkably used in bringing revival in New England.
Jonathan Edwards was moved to tears because, by
comparison, his own so fruitful ministry seemed to be
unprofitable. He told Thomas Prince that 'there were
very extraordinary effects of Mr. Buell's labours; the
people were exceedingly moved, crying out in great
numbers in the meeting house, and great part of the
congregation commonly staying in the house of God for
hours after the public service.' Who, again, has heard of
Donald Munro? The blind parish catechist of Portree,
on the Isle of Skye, was the medium of uncommon
blessing in the 1812 awakening. He was the means of
establishing prayer groups in many parts of the island and
wherever he went conversions were numerous. Bracadale,
Snizort, Kilmuir, Diurnish—all were signally visited by the
Spirit of God under Munro's ministry. 'It is impossible to
reflect on his career'—so runs the chronicle of this

revival—'without being impressed with the truth that God is "no respecter of persons," and that the distinctions, of which men are apt to make so much, are often lightly set by of Him. He can choose His instruments from the most unlikely materials, and, in performing His works of wonder, strikingly prove that "the excellency of the power is of Himself." He once selected a child of tender years, through whom to speak to His people, passing by a regularly appointed and aged servant; and not more forcibly did He then announce, than He has done among us, by the history of Donald Munro: "Them that honour Me I will honour, and they that despise Me shall be lightly esteemed".'

This same mystery is reflected in the accompaniments of revival. As the sceptics are only too eager to remind us, revival may lead to displays of emotion and occasionally of physical violence which would hardly seem to indicate the influence of the Holy Spirit, but rather of some demoniac power. In every awakening, apparently, the precious is mingled with the vile. It was not long after Pentecost before Simon Magus sought, like a new and even more daring Prometheus, to steal the heavenly fire and capitalise it for his own pernicious purposes. And it would seem that seasons of spiritual renewal rouse the Devil to his most sinister devices. He is the father of lies and has an infernal counterfeit to set against every move-ment of the Spirit. As Dora Greenwell has written, with genuine insight, 'We shall scarcely ever find any deep spiritual awakening in any community or in any heart which is not attended and sometimes warped by counter-acting developments, also spiritual, in which we may trace signs that look like the dark and terrible irony of a being whose hatred to the human race is so deadly that he will, if possible, work man's woe through his very blessedness.' It is at this point that the mystery of the

Spirit's operation reaches its most inexplicable culmination and we can only bow before the Divine wisdom which permits the holiest so to flourish alongside the most satanic.

REVIVAL IS MYSTERIOUS IN ITS OBJECTIVE. The end is hid deep in the counsels of God. Revival leads we know not where. It is like the wind. We cannot tell whither it goes. It brushes the hilltops, whistles through the valleys and then departs to a destination unspecified.

So it is with revival. The consequences are quite incalculable. Sometimes Christians are puzzled because God's gracious visitations seem so short. They seldom endure for long. Martin Luther used to say that a religious quickening always exhausted itself within thirty years. Why does revival fade so soon? That is a query that will occupy us in the next chapter, but meanwhile we have to confess that the ceasing of the manna is part of the mystery that enfolds the Spirit's activity. The answer is concealed in the unfathomable abyss of Deity. But one important consideration must be borne in mind. It is this: that though a revival may come to a halt, its repercussions are felt for many years to follow. The floodtide may be past, but the fruit remains in the life and witness of men and women who have been touched and transformed by its influence. Alexander Whyte is a case in point. He spread blessing and transmitted the fulness of the Spirit long after the '59 revival had died down.

We will therefore finish as we began with a quotation from Dr. Whyte. It as as relevant to us today as it was when he uttered it. May it stir us to renewed endeavour and incessant intercession 'until the Spirit be poured upon us from on high, and the wilderness be a fruitful field, and the fruitful field be counted for a forest' (Isaiah 32. 15). 'Go on and preach His Gospel, for He has it in His seven-sealed book that there will be a time of refreshing till all the ends of the earth shall see the salvation of God. See that you are doing your utmost to hasten on that kingdom. For whatever else is shipwrecked on the face of God's earth the kingdom of the Lord Jesus Christ is sure to come into harbour . . .

> "For Thou art God that dost
> To me salvation send,
> And I upon Thee all the day
> Expecting do attend."

CHAPTER XV

THE DECLINE OF REVIVAL

'Quench not the Spirit.'   —I Thessalonians 5. 19

IN his *Confessions and Retractions* that eccentric figure of the New England awakening, James Davenport, expressed the somewhat forlorn hope that his adjuration would destroy the prejudices against Christianity in general and 'the *late* glorious work of God in particular' that had been aroused largely through his own misguided behaviour. This was in 1744. Within two short if memorable years the revival had been brought to an end as sudden and at first sight as inexplicable as its beginning. A merely human assessment of the situation might decide that it had run itself to a standstill. On the other hand, a theological reason could be found in the inscrutable decrees of Almighty God. But there is an area of truth to be explored in relation to the decline of revival which lies in the uncharted territory between these two explanations, and to this task we turn our attention now.

It is a saddening enquiry. It would be much more congenial to sidetrack it altogether. It pains us to realise that the splendour of revival fades. Even though the blessed influences remain, it cannot be pretended that the historical awakenings of the Church have proved permanent. No realistic account of revival can afford to shirk the fact. There are those, of course, who do not expect the spiritual glow to be maintained. Such a stalwart as William Cooper of Boston ventured this prognostication early in 1741. 'The present season is indeed extraordinary. We have enjoyed some new, powerful, and impressive means of grace. Many have been wrought upon. There are many examples of persons in concern for their souls, and striving after salvation. Religion, and especially the nature and necessity of conversion, is now much more the subject of conversation than has been usual. But as these things become more familiar, and the occasion begins to grow old, it may be expected the concern of some will abate; and their convictions, though now seemingly great, will gradually decay, and at length go off; and they will appear to be such manner of persons as they were before. I tell you of this before it comes to pass, that you may not be offended.' As a shrewd calculation from previous instances, such a warning may be justifiable, but are we therefore to conclude that the new life God gives is no more likely to survive than the transient emotions of men? Dr. MacFarlan of Renfrew, who wrote about the eighteenth century awakening in Scotland, came to the conclusion that the proper end of a revival does not require that it should continue. 'One of the most common objections to such seasons is that they are temporary,' he said. 'And so ought they,' he went on. 'A soul asleep in sin has to be awakened, so as to think of its condition, and be led to Christ; but being awakened, it has only to be kept awake, not to be awakened anew in the same way as before. A church is different in this, that, for the sake of awakening sinners, it has itself to be from time to time awakened; but it would not do, even for a church, to be always in the condition of Cambuslang in 1742 and 1743.' That would appear to be a strange deduction to draw from the premises the author had already laid down. A church, like a soul, has to be kept awake, and that in itself demands the perpetuation of Pentecost. But a church, unlike a soul, is never the same entity from one year to another, and therefore stands in double need of continual quickening. And if that be true of the local church, how much more true it is of the Church Universal. We can only conclude, therefore, that the people of God must be kept in a condition of continuous revival if God's fullest purpose in and through them is to be fulfilled. If this indeed be so, then we can hardly regard the decline of revival as inevitable or believe that it is God's will that His children should lose the blessing. And as to discussions on 'how a revival should be brought to a close' (to quote a subheading in a much-used textbook on the subject), we must assume that such a question could only arise where the real nature of Pentecostal awakening has been seriously misconceived.

There is surely a world of difference between the frank acknowledgment that in fact in the past revival always *has* declined and the unscriptural and unauthorised assertion that it always *must* decline. The distinguishing feature of Pentecost was the bestowal of the Holy Spirit upon the Church no longer as an intermittent visitor but as an abiding Guest. God the Father intended the Comforter to dwell with the people of God for ever. If His power be withdrawn (for His presence will never again be taken from us), it is much more probable that the reason lies in the failure of believers than in the arbitrary counsel of God. That indeed is what the Scripture itself teaches. And so, in the context of the Church and immediately prior to a caution against despising the manifestations of Pentecost, the apostle Paul pleads with the Thessalonians not to quench the Spirit. This, according to William Burns, is 'the great and summing evil' with reference to the season of revival. Here is the sad explanation for the departure of glory. This is why revival declines.

The verb 'to quench' is an interesting one. It means to

damp down a fire. Our Lord employed the same word when He quoted Isaiah 42. 3 and identified Himself with the Suffering Servant who would not snuff out the dimly burning wick of a candle (cf. Matthew 12. 20). It is found in Ephesians 6. 16 where Paul, in describing the Christian's armour, tells us that the shield of faith can extinguish all the fire-tipped missiles of the Wicked One. It occurs in Hebrew 11. 34 where it indicates how the heroes of faith subdued the violence of fire—doubtless a reference to the three Hebrew children in Nebuchadnezzar's furnace (cf. Daniel 3. 25). In the passive, it appears in Matthew 25. 8 in the complaint of the foolish bridesmaids that their lamps had gone out and negatively in Mark 9. 44, 46, 48 to depict the indestructible fires of hell. Here in 1 Thessalonians 5. 19 the Holy Spirit is obviously regarded under the image of fire, as so often elsewhere in God's Word. John the Baptist had declared concerning Christ, 'He shall baptise you with the Holy Ghost and with fire' (Matthew 3. 11), and on the day of Pentecost tongues like as of fire rested upon each of the apostolic band. To quench the Spirit is thus to stamp out the Pentecostal fire. It is to smother and suppress the working of the Holy Ghost. In short, it is to put an end to revival. The Scripture informs us that the Spirit can be resisted (Acts 7. 51) and warns us against grieving Him by sin (Ephesians 4. 31). But, worst of all, He can be quenched. A fire may be put out by being overlaid: the Spirit can be quenched when the Church is choked with cares and riches and pleasures. A fire may be put out by negligence: the Spirit can be quenched when believers fail to stir up the gift of God. A fire may be put out by lack of air: the Spirit can be quenched by the absence of spirituality within the Christian fellowship. The consequences of thus sinning against the Holy Ghost are necessarily grave. 'But they rebelled, and vexed His

Holy Spirit: therefore He was turned to be their enemy, and He fought against them' (Isaiah 63. 10).

It is thus just as unwise and unscriptural to suppose that revival cannot be hindered as to believe that it must needs decline. Everything hinges upon the relationship of the Church to the Holy Spirit. If the Spirit is not quenched, there is no reason why revival should not be continuous. But the chastening evidence of history is that every recorded awakening has been brought to an eventual halt because in some way the Spirit has been quenched. We shall do well to weigh some of the factors which tend to dissipate revival and cause the Holy Dove to mourn. They are not irrelevant to a period like our own when the vision tarries, for the sins that nullify revival also prevent its emergence.

Revival declines through THE WANING OF ZEAL. At the heart of any retrogression in the work of God there lies a fatal decrease of enthusiasm amongst the people of His choice. The spiritual temperature drops: the fire of the Spirit dies down: the Pentecostal energy subsides. Everything tends to return to the deadly normal. Revival has come to an end because believers are no longer zealously affected in a good thing (Galatians 4. 18).

In his sermon on 'The More Excellent Way,' John Wesley discusses the reasons why the primitive Church forgot its first love and forfeited the gifts of the Spirit. 'The cause was not, as has been vulgarly supposed, "because there was no more occasion for them," all the world having become Christian. This is a miserable mistake; not a twentieth part of it was then nominally Christian. The real cause was "the love of many," almost of all Christians, so called, was "waxed cold." The Christians had no more of the Spirit of Christ than the other heathens. The Son of Man, when He came to examine His Church, could hardly find "faith upon earth." This was the real cause why the extraordinary gifts of the Holy Ghost were no longer to be found in the Christian Church; because the Christians were turned heathen again, and had only a dead form left.' Such a relapse always makes for the decline of revival.

Nowhere does the waning of zeal reveal itself more tragically than in the realm of prayer. When the pressure of prevailing intercession is reduced, the tide of blessing begins to ebb. We have seen how closely prayer is related to the advent of revival: it is equally associated with the maintenance of revival. If the intensity of Gethsemane pleadings is relaxed even for a brief space, the work of the Spirit is immeasurably hampered. James Robe of Kilsyth lamented this very thing as he wrote in 1749: 'Had the concert (i.e. of prayer) been renewed which had begun about 1744, who can tell but that the revival would have been much more extensive and continuous?' In his *History of Primitive Methodism* Hugh Bourne complained that in 1817 and 1818 the camp meetings were losing their power and that the converting work had almost ceased in them. This he attributed to the growing custom of holding the camp-meetings 'almost altogether with preachings and cutting off the general praying services.' When prayer was once again set in the central place, 'the Lord returned in mercy, restored the converting power to the camp-meetings, and . . . the circuit began to revive.'

A thorough scrutiny of the relevant materials corroborates the sound judgment of Dr. Arthur T. Pierson when he remarked that 'from the Day of Pentecost, there has been not one great spiritual awakening in any land which has not begun in a union of prayer, though only among two or three; no such outward, upward movement has continued after such prayer meetings have declined; and it is in exact proportion to the maintenance of such joint and believing supplication and intercession that the

Word of the Lord in any land or locality has had free course and been glorified.'

Revival declines through THE SLACKENING OF DISCIPLINE. The Church is an ordered society. It has received governmental authority from Christ the Head for the express purpose of ensuring the efficiency of its regulative oversight and the purity of its fellowship. Hence the Church reproves, rebukes, exhorts, 'lest any root of bitterness springing up trouble' the flock of Christ 'and thereby many be defiled' (Hebrews 12. 15).

It is especially necessary that in a time of awakening the discipline of the Church should be exercised with diligent firmness. Believers will be encouraged to self-denial and cross-bearing in obedience to our Lord's command. Where this martyr spirit is absent, revival declines. 'When the church has enjoyed a revival, and begins to grow fat upon it, and runs into self-indulgence,' says Finney, 'the revival will soon cease. Unless they sympathise with the Son of God, Who gave up all to save sinners; unless they are willing to give up their luxuries, and their ease, and lay themselves out in the work, they need not expect the Spirit of God will be poured out upon them. This is undoubtedly one of the principal causes of personal declension. Let Christians in a revival beware, when they first find an inclination creeping upon them to shrink from self-denial, and to give in to one self-indulgence after another. It is the device of Satan, to bait them off from the work of God, and make them dull and gross, and lazy, and fearful, and useless, and sensual, and drive away the Spirit and destroy the revival.'

The maintenance of discipline will also ensure that offences are not tolerated within the Church. Nothing more seriously hinders the progress of revival and is likelier to jeopardise its prospects than the condoning of scandals in the Christian community. Our blessed Lord did not anticipate that the visible Church would remain free from worldly contamination. 'It must needs be that offences come' He affirmed, but added with awful emphasis, 'woe to that man by whom the offence cometh!' (Matthew 18. 6). It is the Church's solemn prerogative to preserve its integrity by removing every stumbling-block of Satan that may obtrude itself into the fellowship of the Spirit. Failure to act with prompt decisiveness may well bring revival to an abrupt conclusion. The neglect to purge the Church is deliberate disobedience to Christ Who is the Head, Whose office it is to dispense the influences of the Spirit. 'Suppose ye then that He will sanction a virtual contempt of His authority by pouring down the blessing of His grace?' Dr. Sprague pertinently enquires. 'Suppose ye that, if a church set at naught the rules which He has prescribed, and not only suffer sin, but the grossest sin, in her members, to go unreproved, He will crown all this dishonour done to His Word, all this inconsistency and flagrant covenant-breaking, with a revival of religion? No, brethren, this is not the manner of Him who rules King in Zion. He never loses sight of the infallible directory, which He has given to His Church; and if any portion of His Church lose of it, it is at the peril of His displeasure. Disobedience to His commandments may be expected always to incur His frown; and that frown will be manifested at least by withholding the influences of His grace.'

Revival declines through THE INTRUSION OF CONTROVERSY. It always flourishes when brotherly love prevails and, conversely, it is endangered and ultimately banished when doubtful disputations rend the seamless robe of Christian unity. Satan's most cunning stratagem in his onslaught on the Church is to divide and rule. 'There is one body, and one Spirit, even as ye are called in one hope of your calling, one Lord, one faith, one baptism, one God and Father of all, who is above all, and through all, and in you all' (Ephesians 4. 4-6). We must therefore endeavour 'to keep the unity of the Spirit in the bond of peace' (v. 3) and where this objective is vitiated by factiousness and strife, revival is hindered and halted.

The great awakening in New England was hastened to an early end because of doctrinal and ecclesiastical disagreements. Those who supported the movement were dubbed New Lights whilst those who opposed it were known as Old Lights. 'Such distinguished names of reproach,' Jonathan Edwards commented with regret, 'do as it were divide us into two armies, separated and drawn up in battle array, ready to fight with one another; which greatly hinders the work of God.' The initial fervour of the Methodist revival in England began to dwindle when Wesley and Whitefield reached a theological deadlock which led to what Ronald Knox calls 'the parting of friends.' An uneasy truce was patched up after Wesley had preached his forthright sermon on 'Free Grace' in 1739, but in 1770, on the death of Whitefield, the controversy broke out again with renewed vigour, to say nothing of vituperation, and did much to neutralise the beneficial effects of the revival and to check its steady flow. 'Wherever our lamentable divisions prevailed,' wrote Robe with reference to the Scottish movement of the same period, 'serious religion declined to a shadow. The work of conversion went but slowly and indiscernibly on. The influences of the Holy Spirit were restrained.' The mission of Evan Roberts in Liverpool was almost wrecked by the disunity of the churches and the blessing that had set Wales afire did not break in whilst sectarian rivalry was rife. With admonitory consistency this self-same factor re-appears in the ebbing tide of every revival. Only when brotherly love continues amongst Christians of every persuasion does the experience of Pentecost prolong itself.

A slogan of the Fulton Street Noon Prayer Meeting in New York, which was sustained in all its original intensity throughout the second evangelical awakening in America, read simply: 'No Controverted Points Discussed.' 'The meetings were noted for their catholicity,' says Dr. J. Edwin Orr. 'Leaders were chosen from every evangelical faith, from Baptists, Congregationalists, Episcopalians, Friends, Lutherans, Methodists, Presbyterians, Reformed and the like, with utter impartiality. All were invited, and all were welcome. No man was asked to what regiment he belonged, or from what country he came; but if he fought under the great Captain of Salvation and spoke the language of Canaan, there was room for him. . . . Generally, Christians present were more disposed to consider things held in common than things in disagreement. The interdenominational harmony was splendid, and contributed in no small way to the success of the movement. Partisan views were forgotten in the urge to rescue perishing souls.' That is the atmosphere in which revival is born and kept alive.

Many other factors contributing to the decline of revival might well be considered did space permit— the weakening of faith, the undermining of experience, the blight of ecclesiasticism, the neglect of the Word, the infiltration of pride—but the three mentioned above represent constantly recurring hindrances against which the Church needs to be perpetually on guard. There are lessons here for our own situation. What brings revival to an end also bars the way to its coming, and we must therefore seek to remove these barriers to blessing. Let nothing in our hearts or in our assemblies defer the day when 'the right hand of the Lord is exalted: the right hand of the Lord doeth valiantly' (Psalm 118. 16).

CHAPTER XVI

THE CHALLENGE OF REVIVAL

*'Sow to yourselves in righteousness, reap in mercy; break up
your fallow ground: for it is time to seek the Lord, till He come
and rain righteousness upon you.'*   —Hosea 10. 12

IN the series of messages contained in this book we have
sought to expound the Scripture teaching about
revival and to illustrate it from the records of history.
We have considered every major aspect of the Spirit's
quickening from its gracious promise to its sad decline.
It remains to hear the conclusion of the whole matter as it
affects the people of God today. In this hour of crisis and
opportunity, what is the Spirit saying to the churches in
relation to revival? In the light of what we have learned
from the Scriptures of truth, what must be our immediate
programme? What is the next step ahead? What, in
short, is to be our response to God's challenge in this vital
concern? The answer to that pressing question is nowhere
more clearly provided than in the passage from Hosea
which we are about to examine. Here the Word speaks
in a detailed and specific manner in setting out what
believers are to do before revival descends.

The Jews were a nation of farmers. They were favoured
by the Lord with an exceptionally fertile land, flowing
with milk and honey. Thus their chief occupation was to
till the soil and grow the crops. Just as the Englishman
regards his home as his castle, so the Hebrew ideal of
domestic peace and bliss is expressed in the words of
Micah: 'But they shall sit every man under his vine and
under his fig tree; and none shall make them afraid'
(Micah 4. 4). In view of the fact that agriculture was the

principal industry of Palestine, we are not surprised to discover that the Scripture abounds with allusions to this means of livelihood. This section of Hosea is a case in point. The prophet draws an analogy from the season of harvest and applies it to spiritual fruition.

He addresses himself to the people of God, the nation Israel. Despite the lavish care of the Almighty, 'Israel is an empty vine' (Hosea 10. 1). God's elect have proved unfaithful. They have sinned from the days of Gibeah (v. 9). They have fallen into idolatry, increasing their altars and carving heathen images (v. 1). The prophet arraigns the backsliding citizens of God's own country. He rebukes their lapse into paganism and tells them that God will punish them for their sins. 'It is in My desire that I should chastise them,' says the Lord (v. 10). They have wanted to enjoy the good of the land without working for it. Ephraim was like a heifer that loved to eat the fat of harvest but whose neck had never been bent to the yoke (v. 11). With this vivid illustration Hosea reminds his hearers that there can be no fruit without labour. The price of harvest has to be paid. God's annual gift of replenishment to the tired earth cannot be appropriated without man's toil.

What was relevant to the nation when Hosea prophesied is equally applicable to us today. The Church is the new Israel, the continuing people of God, the heir both to the promises and the warnings of the Old Testament Scripture. 'But ye are a chosen generation,' Peter tells the infant Christian community scattered over Asia Minor and spreading into Europe, 'a royal priesthood, an holy nation, a peculiar people; that ye should shew forth the praises of Him Who called you out of darkness into His marvellous light: which in time past were not a people, but are now the people of God' (1 Peter 2. 9, 10). There is discernible in the Church today a renewed interest in revival. We are looking for a spiritual harvest. We want to witness another Pentecost. We feel the need for an inrush of new life. But when sometimes we talk so excitedly about the day when the heavens are rent and the mountains flow, are we really ready to face the challenge of what it will involve? Sir George Adam Smith noted that verse ten of Hosea Ten reflects 'the ambition of the people for spiritual results without a spiritual discipline.' Is not that the precise condition of the Church in our time? Let us, then, seek to meet the call of revival as we ponder from this text the processes that precede the harvest. We shall rearrange them in their chronological order. This is what must happen before blessing falls. That is not to say that even when every item has been fulfilled that God is then bound to act. The final issue still lies with Him.

The first process in the harvest timetable is PLOUGHING. 'Break up your fallow ground.' This Divine command is so urgent that it is repeated in Jeremiah 4. 3. Fallow ground is that which was once cultivated but now lies waste. It has not gone wild again, but is barren and unproductive because it has not been tilled. The reference is obviously not to the unregenerate, but to the Church and God's people within it. And as we measure the situation today, must we not confess that the vast tracts of fallow ground in the hearts of professing Christians constitute the most substantial hindrance to revival?

The initial response demanded of believers to the challenge of revival is to recognise their own short-coming. That is where revival starts. Before the ground can be fruitful again it needs to be broken up. Often God breaks to make. Only when we are crushed at the Cross can He use us to His glory. The motto of the 1904 revival in Wales was, 'Bend the Church and save the people.' Brokenness, says Norman Grubb, is the keyword to revival. Only when Christians confess sin and are prepared to let the Lord direct their lives in every particular will the channels be clear for blessing to flow. Douglas Brown tells of God's dealing with him when he was to all intents and purposes the highly successful pastor of a London church. Even in the midst of his expanding ministry he was dissatisfied and seeking God's best, though then unwilling to pay the price. He wanted God to use him on his own terms. After four months of battle, he lay broken and empty at the foot of Calvary. Relating that harrowing experience he speaks of God's infinite patience. 'It took Him four months to teach me to say two words: "Lord, anything".' That is what is meant by breaking up the fallow ground. The ploughers have to plough upon our backs and make long their furrows before revival is granted.

The next process in the harvest timetable is SOWING. 'Sow to yourselves in righteousness' says Hosea, and the parallel in Jeremiah has 'sow not among thorns.' That shows quite plainly that we are listing these several stages in accurate order. It is obviously futile to sow without ploughing first of all. Whilst weeds are choking the soil, no seed has a chance to mature. The fallow ground has to be broken up before the seedtime comes.

'Sow to *yourselves*' God commands. We have to sow to others as well: that is evangelism. But we have to sow to ourselves, and that is the way of revival. The seed, of course, is the Word, and the fruit is righteousness. Is the Word of God being sufficiently sown in the hearts of believers today? Are we genuinely eager to hear? Do we hunger for the bread of life? Is the Bible indeed our food and drink? Would we rather miss a meal than omit our daily portion? Is the Lord's Day the best of all the seven because then we can go into God's House and hear the vital Word? Until such questions no longer mock us by their sheer incompatibility with our present condition, there can be no prospect of revival. When they no longer sound incongruous, then the day may be near.

When the Word is sown within, it will bear fruit without. Christians will cease to look just the same as anyone else to the unbeliever. There will be a distinctive quality about their conduct and character. They will be what God wants them to be—'a peculiar people unto Himself' (Deuteronomy 14. 2). Too often Christians are afraid to be different from the rest of mankind. According to Dr. Henry Sloane Coffin, the Eleventh Commandment today is 'Thou shalt not be queer.' Most of us hate to be out of step. And so the excuse of so many Christians when they succumb to conventional morality is expressed in the words of the song, 'Everybody's doing it.' But God demands that we be Daniels. We are to be marked out from the mass because we walk in the Spirit and thus no longer fulfil the lust of the flesh (Galatians 5. 16). That is what is implied by 'sowing to ourselves in righteousness.'

The third process in the harvest timetable is WAITING. 'For it is time to seek the Lord.' And in Hosea 12. 6: 'Therefore turn thou to God: keep mercy and judgment, and wait on thy God continually.' There is still time to cry unto Him. The sands have not yet run out. So, 'Seek ye the Lord while He may be found, call ye upon Him while He is near' (Isaiah 55. 6). Waiting is uncongenial to most of us. We are born activists. We must be up and doing. And we invariably introduce this spirit into the Church and imagine that unless we are bustling about organising something, then we are failing in fidelity. There are times when, like Martha, we must needs be cumbered about with much serving, always abounding in the work of the Lord, but there are other times when we must sit like Mary at the Master's feet and simply wait His leisure.

That is an unavoidable element in the harvest programme. 'Behold, the husbandman waiteth for the
precious fruit of the earth, and hath long patience for it,
until he receive the early and latter rain' (James 5. 7).
Here is one of the profoundest secrets of revival. It is not
to be chased after: it is to be waited for. No amount of
misguided impetuosity of ours will bring it one whit
nearer. Whilst we meet God's requirements we must
nevertheless possess our souls in patience. God's promise
is sure: He will intervene, but not at our signal. We
cannot contrive revival. We must await it from Him.
'Though it tarry, wait for it; because it will surely come,
it will not tarry' (Habakkuk 2. 3).

One of the most striking sections of William Arthur's
The Tongue of Fire is entitled 'The Waiting for the
Fulfilment.' It deals with the period of patient tarrying
before Pentecost. In vivid language the author pictures
the apostles returning from the mount of Ascension in
obedience to their Lord to wait for the gift of the Spirit.
Ten whole days they remained in humble expectancy.
'Wait for the promise of My Father, which, saith He, ye
have heard of Me. For John truly baptised with water;
but ye shall be baptised with the Holy Ghost not many
days hence' (Acts 1. 4, 5). 'Not many days'—but how
long they seemed. 'But the days wear on, and no blessing.
Is not the delay long? "*Not* many days!" Does the
promise hold good? They must have felt disappointed
as the evening fell, and no sign of an answer to their
oft-repeated prayer. Now is the hour of trial. Will their
faith fail? Will some begin to forsake the meetings which
bring not the baptism they seek? Will some stay at home,
or "go a-fishing," saying that they will wait the Lord's
time, and not be unwarrantably anxious about what,
after all, does not depend on them, but on the Lord?
Will no one say—"We have done our duty, and must

leave results. We cannot command the fulfilment of the promise. We have asked for it, asked sincerely, fervently, repeatedly: we can do no more"?' Only after such prayerful, faithful, agonised waiting was the mighty power of Pentecost outpoured. The disciples of our Lord hung on in bare dependence on His word—and at the last their trust and hope had their reward. That is how it must ever be with respect to revival. When we have done all He lays upon us and, indeed, whilst we are continuing so to obey, we must 'rest in the Lord, and wait patiently for Him' (Psalm 37. 7).

Ploughing, sowing, waiting—these are the processes of harvest viewed from the human angle. The next rests altogether with God. It is RIPENING. 'Till He come and rain righteousness upon you.' It is God and God alone who nurtures and matures the grain. 'Where harvests ripen *Thou* art there' and if God were not there harvests would not ripen. The farmer may plant and water, but God gives the increase. '*Till* He come' says the prophet: not *that* He may come, or *then* He will come. The gift is His and cannot be earned by all our strivings. The time is His and cannot be hastened by all our pleadings. Revival is a blessing from God's sovereignty.

It is typified here under the symbolism of rain. In an important chapter of his book *In the Day of Thy Power* Arthur Wallis has expounded the salient Old Testament passages which relate to the latter rain of promise and its bearing on revival. There is a prolonged 'dry season' in Palestine which stretches from April to October. This is broken by what the Scripture calls the 'former rain' The farmer is dependent upon it for softening the iron-hard soil and making it suitable for ploughing and sowing. These heavy falls are followed by many weeks of intermittent showers. Then, as harvest time draws near, the 'latter rain' or rain of ingathering, helps to swell the grain prior to the season of reaping. 'Let us now fear the Lord our God, that giveth rain, both the former and the latter, in his season: He reserveth unto us the appointed weeks of the harvest' (Jeremiah 5. 24). Mr. Wallis regards Pentecost as the spiritual fulfilment of the former rain and believes that before the return of Christ we may expect 'a season of mighty outpourings, eclipsing all that the Church has experienced since the Reformation, and only comparable in character and in power with the former rain of the early Church.' Meanwhile, within the Church age we can look for scattered showers such as continued at intervals throughout the Jewish winter, for we are told that at no period do they cease altogether. It is thus that the Lord will 'come and rain righteousness' upon His people. This is how ripening will set in.

We must refrain from speculation beyond the disclosures of the Word and beware of pretending to a knowledge of times and seasons which the Father hath put in His own power (Acts 1. 7), yet nevertheless we cannot ignore the signs on the prophetic horizon which at least suggest that we are approaching the end of the Gospel age. If there is to be a great ingathering of souls before the Lord's glorious Advent, it is abundantly evident that nothing short of a world-wide revival will accomplish it. The latter rain is a sheer necessity if the earth is to be ripe unto the final harvest. Mercy drops round us are falling, but we must plead for the showers and ultimately for the torrential downpour. 'Ask ye of the Lord rain in the time of the latter rain; so the Lord shall make bright clouds, and give them showers of rain, to every one grass in the field' (Zechariah 10. 1).

And so the final stage is reached, which is REAPING. 'Sow to yourselves in righteousness, reap in mercy,' says Hosea. 'In due season we shall reap, if we faint not' (Galatians 6. 9). The harvest will eventually be gathered when the farmer has worked and waited. So it is with regard to revival. God has ordained that there shall be seasons of rich fecundity and we may therefore confidently hope for more. Faith dares to claim the fulness now. 'Say not ye, There are yet four months, and then cometh the harvest? behold I say unto you. Lift up your eyes, and look on the fields; for they are white already to harvest' (John 4. 35).

The reaping will be in mercy. That means in God's steadfast love. The word stands for God's fidelity to His covenant. Great is His faithfulness and therefore we can unhesitatingly expect to reap. The reaping will also be according to the measure of mercy. God is rich in mercy, says the Scripture (Ephesians 2. 4). He has an abundant supply. And out of that inexhaustible treasury He pours out His blessing. What is reaped in the day of glad ingathering will be in proportion to the manifold mercies of God. Furthermore, the fact that we are able to reap at all will emerge from the mercy of our heavenly Father. All the glory will be His. Revival constrains us to exclaim with Charles Wesley: ''Tis mercy all, immense and free!'

This, then, is the harvest programme. These are the stages that lead up to the climax. Here is the challenge of revival. We rejoice in the prospect, but are we prepared for the costly prerequisites? Are we breaking up our fallow ground? Are we sowing to ourselves in righteousness? Are we seeking the Lord? In the searching words of Charles G. Finney: 'If God should ask you this moment, by an audible voice from heaven, "Do you want a revival?" would you dare to say, Yes? "Are you willing to make the sacrifices?" would you answer, Yes? "When shall it begin?" would you answer, Let it begin today— let it begin here—let it begin in my heart *now*?'

Although we have spoken much, and rightly so, about

the Church in these talks on revival, we dare not overlook the challenging fact that in the last analysis spiritual quickening is a personal affair. God does not operate in a vacuum and the Church is no more than the sum of individual believers. If He is to revive His people the Lord will have to start with someone. Let us each determine that we shall be in the line of blessing because we hold nothing back from Him. May we be willing in the day of His power.

> 'I saw a human life, ablaze with God;
>   I felt a power Divine,
> As through an empty vessel of frail clay
>   I saw God's glory shine.
> Then woke I from a dream, and cried aloud:
>   "My Father, give to me
> The blessing of a life consumed by fire,
>   Let me burn out for Thee"!'

Dr. Reuben A. Torrey was signally used by God as he carried on the great work of Dwight L. Moody. It was through reading Finney's autobiography and the life of George Müller that as a young minister he gave himself without reserve to the Saviour's service. As the pressing need for Pentecostal awakening weighed more and more heavily upon him he was constrained to plead for a further manifestation of the Spirit in his time. But there was nothing conveniently vague or impersonal about his prayer. He drew an imaginary ring around himself on the floor and cried, 'O Lord, send a great revival and begin it in this circle!' That should be the earnest desire of us all. The refining fire must go through *my* heart before it can reach an impotent Church and an indifferent world.